Think,
Write,
Publish

Benjamin Chapin

THINK
WRITE
PUBLISH

How to self-publish a book
Pre-writing, Writing, publishing & Marketing Guide

BENJAMIN CHAPIN

Think, Write, Publish

DEDICATION

Dedicated to my mother,

the woman who taught me

that all things are possible with God.

CONTENTS

ACKNOWLEDGMENTS

First and foremost, I want to thank God. God's salvation through the death, burial and resurrection of Jesus Christ gives us all the ability to have a personal relationship with the creator of the Universe.

I also want to thank my wife. She's my muse and my inspiration. A wonderful wife, an amazing mother and the best person I have ever met. She's great and has always stood by me with every decision I have made along life's way.

I'd like to thank my editors and early readers for helping me along the way. I also want to thank all of my friends and extended family for the support. It's a true blessing to have every person I know in my life.

.

A NOTE FROM THE AUTHOR

EVERY GREAT BOOK STARTS WITH a single word. I've been writing for years, but before that change happened I was an ordinary 9-5er. Self-publishing changed my life and I now have the freedom to live anywhere I want (kind of—kids keep me where I'm at), work in my underwear and take lots of naps. What I found in writing is more than I could have ever dreamed. It's simply divine. I feel blessed by God to have the opportunity to do what I do every day (naps included). My hope for you with this book is this: To equip you with everything you need to succeed in writing and publishing your own works of either fiction or nonfiction. In the front of this book, you'll find what I call "road maps" and they are the absolute best way to navigate the waters of self-publishing and your own journey.

I've read a lot of writing books but have found there's always something that is missing in each one of them—how to *really* do it. For example, one of the biggest parts I find missing in the writing books I've read is the "pre-writing" stage that takes place for someone. I'm not talking about plotting, but instead, I'm talking about finding the time, energy, and passion that drives a story or nonfiction to completion. Many people struggle not with having an idea for a book, but actually writing the book. This book covers it all.

While this book is primarily for fiction writers, the vast majority of the information can be helpful to even the nonfiction writers out there too. No matter what your goals and aspirations are when it comes to writing, I hope my advice helps you get where you want to be.

ROAD MAPS

A QUICK NOTE

SELF-PUBLISHING IS NOT A one size fits all. When I began writing this book, I thought it was just a basic how-to for publishing until I realized it's the book I would have *loved* when I started out years ago. This turned into the book that would have saved me years of work and research. I hope it does the same for you.

Each road map is designed to help a specific type of person who might be wishing to publish. There's a road map for the busy stay-at-home mom who just wants a couple extra hundred dollars a month to loosen up the budget. There's one for a business person seeking to add a book to their list of accomplishment, experts in fields who need credibility and feel a book might help bring that to their name, people who want to write a book they've had sitting on their desk as a finished manuscript; the list goes on and on. Be sure to pick one of these maps and follow it. I won't promise you the world, but I will promise you'll get that book or those books published.

Each section will give you a quick overview of who it's designed for, and then you'll be able to decide if it's the right map for you. Step-by-step instructions are included in each map to help you. My hope is that you find it enjoyable and are able to find success on your journey. Please e-mail me and let me know if you get your book published. I'd love to hear from you (tk@tkchapin.com). Each road map is also available for download at benjaminchapin.com/writing-tools/.

Benjamin Chapin

THE DUSTY MANUSCRIPT

A PERSON WITH A STORY to tell. This type of person has one story they've rewritten a dozen different times and have probably even shown it to a few select individuals.

Everybody loves it, but they've been scared to take that first step.

If this sounds like you, I want to tell you right now, just picking up this book was the first step in the right direction. I'm going to help you from start to finish with publishing it, and I'm even going to recommend where you can promote it afterward (that is based on my own experiences). Welcome to publishing.

1. Congratulations on finishing a manuscript! Getting it done is a big portion of the battle. Now, it's time to get that thing edited.

2. Read the following sections located in CHAPTER 10 FINE-TUNING THE MANUSCRIPT: BETA READERS, LINE EDITOR, PROOFREADERS and get busy!

3. Read CHAPTER 11 FORMATTING. This will take care of all the information you need to properly format your e-book and paperback.

4. Before you publish, you need to send out early copies. Go ahead and read CHAPTER 14 NOW GIVE IT AWAY: Advance Reading Copies (ARCs).

5. While you're waiting for your ARCs to be read, you should set up your website. You should read CHAPTER 21 AUTHOR WEBSITES, CHAPTER 19 LET'S GET SOCIAL, CHAPTER 12 BOOK COVERS, and CHAPTER 22 E-MAIL MARKETING.

6. You should now have all your social profiles in place, a book cover, your manuscript formatted, your website up and running, and your mailing list ready to go! Now, it's time to publish (usually a week or two after ARCs went out. Try to work around the schedules of those who have it for maximized impact). Read CHAPTER 15 KEYWORDS AND YOU, CHAPTER 16 PAGE OPTIMIZATION, CHAPTER 19 AMAZON PROMOTIONS INFORMATION, and CHAPTER 13 HOW TO PUBLISH THE BOOK

7. Once published, allow it to fully publish (Amazon will e-mail you letting you know it's ready) and then go ahead and send the Amazon link out to the people who received the ARCs (so they can leave a review).

8. Now that you're done, it's time to pump the promotion machine. Read CHAPTER 17 FREE PROMOTIONS and CHAPTER 18 PAID PROMOTIONS

9. Continue to find readers on Goodreads even after publication and offer your book in exchange for an honest review. Each person who falls in love with your book is a potential future customer or will, at least, tell others. Keep growing and pushing forward.

10. Congratulations! Now, write another book!

THE PART-TIME INCOME SEEKER

EVER BEEN JUST A FEW dollars short at the end of payday and hated it? Maybe you want some extra money to go on vacation, pay off some debt, or maybe even fund a new boat. Whatever the case is, this path is for you. This road map has been designed to fit you exactly.

Welcome to publishing.

1. You're going to need motivation to keep going on this journey, so I recommend starting at the beginning of this book: CHAPTER 1 CULTIVATING THE WHY, CHAPTER 2 PASSIONATE WRITING, CHAPTER 3 FINDING TIME, CHAPTER 4 IDEA GENERATING MACHINE, and CHAPTER 5 GOAL-SETTING FOR SUCCESS

2. Once you have an idea in mind, it's time to get writing. This part will take you the longest, but do not give up. You can and will do this. Stay focused and dedicated. Read CHAPTER 6 CREATING AN EXPERIENCE, CHAPTER 7 WHEN & WHERE TO WRITE, and CHAPTER 8 FURST DRAFFS SUK. Once you've done that, write and don't stop until it's done.

3. Go ahead and read: CHAPTER 9 REVISE, CRY, REVISE.

4. Read the following sections located in CHAPTER 10 FINE-TUNING THE MANUSCRIPT: BETA READERS, LINE EDITOR, PROOFREADERS and get busy!

5. Read CHAPTER 11 FORMATTING. This will take care of all the information you need to properly format your e-book and paperback.

6. Before you publish, you need to send out early copies. Go ahead and read CHAPTER 14 NOW GIVE IT AWAY: Advance Reading Copies (ARCs).

7. While you're waiting for your ARCs to be read, you should set up your website. Read CHAPTER 21 AUTHOR WEBSITES, CHAPTER 20 LET'S GET SOCIAL, CHAPTER 12 BOOK COVERS, and CHAPTER 22 E-MAIL MARKETING.

8. You should now have all your social profiles in place, a book cover, your manuscript formatted,

your website up and running, and your mailing list ready to go! Now it's time to publish (usually a week or two after ARCs went out. Try to work around the schedules of those who have it for maximized impact). Read CHAPTER 15 KEYWORDS AND YOU, CHAPTER 16 PAGE OPTIMIZATION, CHAPTER 19 AMAZON PROMOTIONS INFORMATION, and CHAPTER 13 HOW TO PUBLISH THE BOOK

9. Once published, allow it to fully publish and once the link is available, go ahead and send it out to the people who received the ARCs.

10. Now that you're done, it's time to pump the promotion machine. Read CHAPTER 17 FREE PROMOTIONS, and CHAPTER 18 PAID PROMOTIONS

11. Continue to find readers on Goodreads even after publication and offer your book in exchange for an honest review. Each person who falls in love with your book is a potential future customer or will, at least, tell others. Keep growing and pushing forward.

12. Congratulations! Now write another book!

THE FULL-TIME DREAMER

SO YOU WANT TO WRITE for a living? Awesome! It's going to take a lot of work, but with dedication, hard work, and continuous re-analyzing of your systems and routines, you'll be on your way to a full-time income.

Welcome to publishing.

1. You're going to need motivation to keep going on this journey, so I recommend starting at the

beginning of this book: CHAPTER 1 CULTIVATING THE WHY, CHAPTER 2 PASSIONATE WRITING, CHAPTER 3 FINDING TIME, CHAPTER 4 IDEA GENERATING MACHINE, and CHAPTER 5 GOAL-SETTING FOR SUCCESS

2. Once you have an idea in mind, it's time to get writing. This part will take you the longest, but do not give up. You can and will do this. Stay focused and dedicated. Read CHAPTER 6 CREATING AN EXPERIENCE, CHAPTER 7 WHEN & WHERE TO WRITE, and CHAPTER 8 FURST DRAFFS SUK. Once you've done that, write and don't stop until it's done.

3. Go ahead and read CHAPTER 9 REVISE, CRY, REVISE.

4. Read the following sections located in CHAPTER 10 FINE-TUNING THE MANUSCRIPT: BETA

READERS, LINE EDITOR, PROOFREADERS and get busy!

5. Read CHAPTER 11 FORMATTING. This will take care of all the information you need to properly format your e-book and paperback.

6. Before you publish, you need to send out early copies. Go ahead and read CHAPTER 14 NOW GIVE IT AWAY: Advance Reading Copies (ARCs).

7. While you're waiting for your ARCs to be read, you should set up your website. Read CHAPTER 21 AUTHOR WEBSITES, CHAPTER 20 LET'S GET SOCIAL, CHAPTER 12 BOOK COVERS, and CHAPTER 22 E-MAIL MARKETING.

8. You should now have all your social profiles in place, a book cover, your manuscript formatted, your website up and running, and your mailing list ready to go! Now it's time to publish (usually a

week or two after ARCs went out. Try to work around the schedules of those who have it for maximized impact). Read CHAPTER 15 KEYWORDS AND YOU, CHAPTER 16 PAGE OPTIMIZATION, CHAPTER 19 AMAZON PROMOTIONS INFORMATION, and CHAPTER 13 HOW TO PUBLISH THE BOOK. Also, be sure to pay attention to the multiple options for publishing. Audiobooks and paperbacks can ramp up your income and get you that much closer to a full-time income.

9. Once published, allow it to fully publish and once the link is available, go ahead and send it out to the people who received the ARCs.

10. Now that you're done, it's time to pump the promotion machine. Read CHAPTER 17 FREE

PROMOTIONS, and CHAPTER 18 PAID PROMOTIONS.

11. Continue to find readers on Goodreads even after publication and offer your book in exchange for an honest review. Each person who falls in love with your book is a potential future customer or will, at least, tell others.

12. When you start to see reviews come in, read them all. Analyze what your readers are saying. What's good, what's bad, and what's utter poop. Your readers are going to be the ones who support you as a full-time writer, so you better make them happy. Take these bad reviews to heart when the criticism is merited. This will separate you from the rest of the people. Ignore the downright nasty reviews, but take to heart the improvements that can be made moving forward.

13. If you didn't particularly enjoy the genre of your first book, start on a different one. It can take you some time to find the perfect niche (category or term for genre of writing), so keep attempting new titles. It took me a year-and-a-half to figure out what genre I was going to be in but once I did, I knew it and cut away all the rest of the titles under that pseudonym so I could appear an expert in that one.

14. Congratulations! Now write another book!

THE EXPERT

IF YOU'RE SOMEONE WHO NEEDS to write a book that goes alongside your already established company, career, or path, this is the road map for you. Getting your book published is the main point of this; you don't need to come up with ideas, you just need to get your content organized, put into words, and published.

Welcome to publishing.

1. You're going to need to read CHAPTER 5 GOAL-SETTING FOR SUCCESS.

2. Since you're already an expert in the field, you might or might not have content ready to get organized. I'll recommend the following based on the fact that you don't have content ready to go. Read CHAPTER 6 CREATING AN EXPERIENCE, CHAPTER 7 WHEN & WHERE TO WRITE, and CHAPTER 8 FURST DRAFFS SUK. Once you've done that, write and don't stop until it's done.

3. Go ahead and read CHAPTER 9 REVISE, CRY, REVISE.

4. Read the following sections located in CHAPTER 10 FINE-TUNING THE MANUSCRIPT: BETA READERS, LINE EDITOR, PROOFREADERS and get busy!

5. Read CHAPTER 11 FORMATTING. This will take care of all the information you need to properly format your e-book and paperback.

6. Before you publish, you need to send out early copies. Go ahead and read CHAPTER 14 NOW GIVE IT AWAY: Advance Reading Copies (ARCs).

7. While you're waiting for your ARCs to be read, you should set up your website, social networks, and find someone to create a book cover (or do it yourself). If you're already an expert, this might or might not pertain to you (depends on what you already have established). You should read CHAPTER 21 AUTHOR WEBSITES, CHAPTER 20 LET'S GET SOCIAL, CHAPTER 12 BOOK COVERS, and CHAPTER 22 E-MAIL MARKETING.

8. You should now have all your social profiles in place, a book cover, your manuscript formatted,

your website up and running, and your mailing list ready to go! Now it's time to publish (usually a week or two after ARCs went out. Try to work around the schedules of those who have it for maximized impact). Read CHAPTER 15 KEYWORDS AND YOU, CHAPTER 16 PAGE OPTIMIZATION, CHAPTER 19 AMAZON PROMOTIONS INFORMATION, and CHAPTER 13 HOW TO PUBLISH THE BOOK

9. Once published, allow it to fully publish and once the link is available, go ahead and send it out to the people who received the ARCs.

10. Now that you're done, it's time to pump the promotion machine. Read CHAPTER 17 FREE PROMOTIONS, and CHAPTER 18 PAID PROMOTIONS

11. Continue to find readers on Goodreads even after publication and offer your book in exchange for an honest review. Each person who falls in love with your book is a potential future customer or will, at least, tell others. Keep growing and pushing forward.

12. Congratulations! Now write another book!

SECTION I: BEFORE WRITING

CHAPTER 1
CULTIVATING THE WHY

IT'S VITAL YOU UNDERSTAND THE "why" that is fueling

you to write the book your heart wishes to write. Ask

yourself: What fuels your desire to write this book in

particular? Is it because you have something to say or

because you saw someone make some money writing

books? Are you passionate about whatever it is you want to

write? Or are you trying to earn a few bucks? Either one is

fine, but it's important to keep your perspective and know why you write.

Finding your motivation is crucial to your long-term success. You don't cross the finish line with half-hearted hopes and dreams. There has to be something that keeps you going when you don't want to go anymore. There has to be something that glues you to your seat for hours upon hours while you bleed onto the pages.

To help you gain perspective on your why I'll tell you the origins of my own personal *why*. My why could be a few different things, but really, there is one moment in my life that I can point at and say, "That's why." I'll never forget that memory. I had a full-time job, health insurance for myself and my family, a car payment, and a place to live. At the time, my wife and I were trying to determine how we were going to come up with a co-pay for a doctor. I was living the so-called American dream, but I couldn't even come up with a co-pay for my daughter to be seen by a doctor. It was in this moment that I realized no matter the salary, no matter the job, no matter what I was doing—as long as I was working for someone else, I'd have an exact amount of income and I'd forever live within those bounds and limits. Sure, I could get incremental raises and if I wasted enough of my life with a company, I might even get a promotion. Each increase would mean my bills would increase, though. A new car, toy, etc. I was wasting my time working for someone else who could cut me at any moment due to a budget decrease instead of investing in myself, in my future. This *why* was born out of hardship, but it was the reason I pushed myself beyond my own abilities.

While this was my why in the beginning, it wasn't what my why ended up being in the long term. I will testify, though, that this particular why was the reason I was able to wake up at 3 a.m. and work on my writing before going to my "9 to 5" job at 7 a.m. It was also the reason I was able to ignore friends and spend weekends and holidays slaving away at my keyboard. That struggle was always in the back of my mind, that *why*.

My why now consists of God and His will for my life. Through writing, I have found my purpose. God has blessed me with an audience that continues to read my stories and my hope is that the stories bless their lives and help illustrate God's power in the lives of believers. In those moments of pain (sixteen hour days and zero to three hours of sleep), I think about the fact the world *needs* these stories. I receive dozens of e-mails monthly from people who have read the stories and tell me how God has affected their life in some way through lessons discovered in the texts. It warms my heart to know God is working in the lives of His believers. Your *why*, the reason you write, will change it. It has to be flexible, fluid and malleable.

When you begin to cultivate your *why*, don't skip it or refuse to give it thought. Your *why* is the backbone of your success in publishing, and it'll help you stay in it for the long haul. Whether you're writing one book or have plans of writing hundreds, you'll need the *why* to keep you going when you don't want to go any longer.

Benjamin Chapin

CHAPTER 2
PASSIONATE WRITING

IF YOU'RE GOING TO WRITE and spend the time required to make something longer than a few paragraphs, it's wise to enjoy what you're writing about. Everybody can recall times in their life (primarily in school) where they had to write something they had no interest writing about. It's grueling, brutal, and downright annoying to the one doing the writing. So, if you don't want to write about 101 awesome chicken recipes, don't do it.

35

When I was a senior in high school, we had to do a project that we were supposed to be working on all throughout the school year. I can recall the evening before a fourteen-page rough draft of my project was due. I was sweating bullets as I hadn't spent any time preparing; I just put it off while everybody else worked on theirs all school year—like one kid who studied sweat in athletes (oh, goody!).

Did I do it? Yes. All I did was write about something I was passionate about in my life at the time—video games.

The passions you have in life are most likely areas in which you have already invested large amounts of time. Using your already established passions will create an anchor point for your writing. The words will flow right onto the page and while you'll still put in a lot of time, it'll be drastically less and definitely more enjoyable when it's rooted in a passion. In this chapter, you will learn how to identify three different types of passion points that you can use to help build your writing anchors. As in life and ourselves, there are three areas that make up the passion points: Body, Soul & Mind.

PASSION: BODY

Do you exercise? Eat healthy? Maybe you're gluten-free? If you have a lifestyle that's built around your body, start writing books in that genre/category (e.g. Paleo dieting). There's no reason why you can't. If you have a special diet because of your health, that could be a reason for writing a book. If your career is in fitness or nutrition, a published book can be an extra income stream and also provide credibility.

PASSION: SOUL

The soul of a human being has no race, no creed, and no boundaries. It's within our souls that dreams come alive and hope resides. Our belief systems live within our souls and it's through the passion of soul and its experience one would find books that span across both nonfiction and fiction. All fiction lives within this category primarily, for all the stories that we tell are to inspire the soul to move in some way. Whether it's fear, happiness, joy, or inspiration, each well-written story moves our soul in a direction and takes us away from where we previously were.

PASSION: MIND

Thinking is one of the most natural things we do as humans. If you're a deeper thinker, enjoy reasoning, or enjoy other how-to types of materials, this might be the category for you. Even if those aren't your forte, chances are no matter what you write, it will tend to tread somewhat into this category from time to time. If you're passionate about cars, how-to books on fixing or troubleshooting car issues could be a great way to get started, for example. Some stories also cause us to stop, think, and analyze our own life. These fiction titles that are able to jump over to this passion are ones you'll read and read again. They'll be the type of book you recommend to friends who might be going through a struggle or a book that deals with a certain struggle that resides in the mind. Many fiction stories will jump between the soul and mind categories of passion.

Many of my own titles such as *Amongst the Flames* are written in hopes to inspire someone struggling in their life. Self-analyzing and re-evaluating what you're doing with your life in all aspects is important in growth and development. Bringing this in a non-threatening way to a reader is brilliant and often a great move if it comes naturally to your writing.

Whether you're writing about a technique you developed to lose weight or the next great American novel, chances are some portion of your passions will trickle into the mind category.

MINING FOR GOLD

Now that you understand the categories your passions reside in, you can begin to mine the gold nuggets that are within you. It's been said that each person has, at least, six books within them that they can write. I believe it's much more than that if they're able to truly dedicate themselves to the craft. With that being said, grab your pickaxe because it's time to start mining.

What do you spend your time doing outside of entertainment (movies and books)? Maybe you enjoy bird watching. Maybe it's thinking. Maybe it's tinkering on an old car.

If you don't have any hobbies outside of entertainment, don't worry. I didn't either, at first. There's no problem with that because oftentimes, we have hidden passions within our life that are just untapped gold mines. It took me over a year to figure out my true passion because it wasn't entirely clear in the beginning.

My passion is my belief in Jesus Christ. While I haven't been the most faithful Christian in regard to prayer, Bible-reading, and church attendance, throughout most of my youth, I have always had a love for the Lord. Cultivating and growing that belief wasn't difficult because I already had a foundation in which to grow.

What is something you a have passion for? Maybe it's web design or photography, or maybe it's creating lesson plans for teachers. Find what you are good at, have an interest in, or care about and cultivate your passion from within it. Spend time carefully discovering the passions you have. You'll learn a lot about yourself.

CHAPTER 3
FINDING TIME

KIDS, SPOUSE, WORK, AND EVERYTHING else don't
simply ask for your time, they demand it. Every time
someone finds out that I write a novel from start to finish
and publish it within a month-and-a-half, their eyes gloss
over and their mouths drop open. They always ask me how I
find the time. Even more unbelievable to them is the fact
that I do more than just write. I spend time with family,
friends, and even take naps most days! How's this possible?

It's all about delegation and priority. I'm not talking about what you do when you're bored, I'm talking about every aspect of your life. Oh, I should also mention I was producing at the same rate when I had a full-time job. I just got up earlier (usually between 3 and 4 a.m.).

My Schedule:

5 a.m. (sometimes 4 a.m.) – Wake up

5 a.m.-6 a.m. – Drink coffee and go over any highly critical tasks (edits, e-mail replies, blog posts, etc. . . .)

7 a.m.-12 p.m. – Write (total writing time: 5 hours)

12 p.m.-1 p.m. – Lunch

1 p.m.-2 p.m. – Nap (or relax)

2:30 p.m.-5 p.m. – Write/Kids (total writing time: up to 2.5 hours)

5 p.m.-6 p.m. – Dinner

6 p.m. – 10 p.m. – Family, friends, work (sometimes— depends on the project and deadlines)

10 p.m. - Sleep

My Schedule (When I worked 40+ hours a week):

3 a.m./4 a.m. – Wake up

4 a.m.-7 a.m. – Drink coffee & write (3 hours of writing)

7 a.m.-5:30 p.m. – Work while listening to writing audiobooks, videos, etc. . . .

5:30 p.m.-6 p.m. – Dinner

6 p.m.-9 or 10 p.m. – Family, relax, work (sometimes— depending on the project)

10 p.m. - Sleep

The thing that probably sticks out most is the early morning. If it wasn't for the sacrifice of sleep, I would have never been able to get to where I am today. I could probably sleep in pretty late now that I don't have a job, but I don't want to. I love what I do and I'm honestly excited to wake up every single day. Sleep is the easiest thing to cut out. You start cutting too much into family time and you risk aggravating the spouse. Sleep is an easy sacrifice. I love sleep, don't get me wrong, but I've learned how to sleep less and get more done.

Important note to the schedules above: You'll notice anytime I have free time I'm writing.

There are days where I just send off a book to an editor and I'm not writing and other days where I'm doing this or that and don't follow it to a tee, but those days will happen. So will the ones where I wake up at 5 a.m. and work all day until midnight. Sleep. And then wake up three hours later to crunch in another jam session to try to meet a deadline. Days in which your eyes feel like they're bleeding and everything is falling apart are the days in which your *why* and a schedule will force you to progress. Without a reason, why would you torture yourself to no end?

You have to sacrifice if you want to get anywhere worthwhile in this life. Maybe it's not sleep, maybe it's *some* of the friendships you have, or maybe it's a favorite TV show. If a person only writes 250 words a day, they'd have an over 91,000-word manuscript in one year's time. That's a pretty awesome realization!

CHAPTER 4
IDEA GENERATING MACHINE

IDEAS ARE A DIME a dozen. Literally, everybody has had

or has ideas in their noggin. Could be book ideas,

inventions, workflows, or whatever. Ideas are cheap. The

quicker you realize that, the quicker you can stop obsessing

over all the amazing ones you have (I've been there, I get it).

If you sit down and apply yourself, you'll discover a never

ending well of ideas.

It's called being human.

Now that we have the realization of ideas being easy to come by, let's get a little deeper. In this chapter, I've compiled some helpful tips and information to help you dig deeper into your stories.

PLOT: TRY WHAT WORKS

If you're struggling for amazing story ideas, think of a novel you have read before that you loved. If you don't want to do that, then just think about an interesting story you've heard. We, as humans, *love* stories, and our ears perk up whenever a story is being told. Everything is within grasp. There are no rules outside of copying another's work (the rule is don't do it!). Please don't copy other people's hard work. I don't care if the story isn't Star Wars because it's called Moon Wars and they have giant noodles they use to fight each other. Don't try to cheat the system. It's a waste of time and you won't benefit anyone.

Instead, let someone's work inspire you to cultivate new ideas. Stay within your genre (if you have one), but explore.

A princess falls in love, but it turns out the man is the prince of the sworn enemy of her father. Awesome. Go ahead and start typing. Make your plot amazing, but don't overthink it. Plotting isn't your story; it's just the framework of the story.

PLOT: THE WORLD AROUND YOU

We live in the information age and we have instant access to lots of information. Included in that is the news. The neat thing about these news organizations is the fact that they do all the heavy lifting for you. You don't even have to do the research; they already have! Oh look, XYZ militant group kills and targets innocent people. Let's spread mass hysteria about it. Not locally, but worldwide. Boom! Write a story about a reporter who was captured by this XYZ group. It's seriously that easy if you're open to it. Or take it a different direction and go with a big nasty group that is starting fires in villages across all the kingdom and killing mayors. You, as an author, are responsible for blurring the lines between reality and fiction.

PLOT: FAMILY, FRIENDS & BEYOND

For the most part, what you find in relationships with family, friends, and spouse as a whole won't be usable material. The reason for this is real life doesn't have to make sense, but fiction does. You have to weave a story that makes sense to the reader and works out in a way that leaves them satisfied.

I've made the mistake of trying to use reality for a story once in my writing career. It was slaughtered in the reviews as unrealistic and horrible. While the reviews made for great comedy, they didn't do so well for the book. It's since been unpublished and tossed in the garbage.

What you can glean from your family, friends, and spouse are little pieces that you can recycle in your writing later. Maybe a situation that happened, maybe a character flaw or character strength or even a mannerism. Also, watch and record bits of information in the back of your mind. Use the people around you as bouts of inspiration. It doesn't matter if you're writing a contemporary romance or a science fiction novel; people are people. Use this fact to your advantage.

PLOT: CRAFTING THE PLOT BASICS

Once you have a rough story idea, get it down to one sentence, if possible. This is crucial in the beginning stages of writing in order to narrow your focus and understand what you're doing for the story. It doesn't need to be pretty to keep your story from running amuck.

Example: A curious boy who lives a mile away from a well falls in.

Once you can narrow it down to one line, you can expand and write a few lines. Be sure to break it down into three parts.

Example: A boy named Miles lives in a small town in Eastern Washington. One day, he goes for a walk and finds that the well he walks by all the time has a glowing, blue light radiating from it. He falls in and is transported to a cartoonish land. He needs to find his way back before supper time if he doesn't want to upset his mother.

The example above contains three separate parts of a story. It's important that you understand where you plan to go with your story. Just like jumping in a boat, you'd better have a destination or you'll just spin around in the harbor. Be sure to understand the basics of the story you want to write, especially in the beginning.

Note: Even beginning discovery writers need to plot basics of a story.

The Three Basics of Story

- Setting/Exposition/Start

- Conflict/Complication/Climax

- Goal/Resolution

Remember, these sentences don't need to be beautiful prose. There's no reason to beat yourself up about how ugly they are or spend any real time on them outside of getting a rough idea of what your story is about. These aren't sentences you need to show anyone. You can show people like your mom, I guess. I'm sure if you were to show her these sentences, she'd be amazed and put them up on her refrigerator. Then, you run the risk of not having your sentences for notes because they're hanging on your mom's fridge. The choice is ultimately up to you, but I'd suggest keeping the sentences under wraps. The more you pull people into the process of writing, the longer it'll take you to progress because of all the additional input.

CHARACTER: USING THE RICH & FAMOUS

An excellent way to anchor your characters is to use the rich and famous. Have a favorite actor? Why? What kind of characteristics do they have? Hop online and watch interviews, take notes on everything about them. What they like, don't like, any quirks, and so on.

Take it a level deeper by studying a specific role in a movie. Did you love that dweeby kid in that one movie? Go watch it and take notes. Use them to flesh out the foundation of your character. Figure out why you like them. This will help you form a list of characteristics that your characters have. This is a trick that will help you write faster stories. While it's good in the beginning of a story, don't force your writing to stay on course with that individual character unless it's absolutely important to your plot. Let your true characters blossom from the foundation you give it.

CHARACTER: USING THE PEOPLE YOU KNOW

Not the type of thing you want to brag about to the people

you're using for inspiration, but an excellent way to build a character. What I often do is latch onto a specific trait that's going to be predominant in the story for that character. This can be a good or bad trait of the character and vital (or not) to your plot. It's all up to you.

I'll tell you about how I did this a specific time. I'll use a fake name to protect the innocent and myself. A man named Craig was a bit of a jerk in real life. What I did for the story I was working on was latch onto a bit of the anger he expressed that I didn't understand. Using that person for the character foundation was the perfect opportunity to not only use him in the story but to see where the character arc (the progression of a character's story) went. He ended up being crushed under a fiery beam of death—and yes, it was satisfying!

SETTING: RESEARCH AND WHAT YOU KNOW

Setting is one of those things that you can waste a lot of time over-researching when you could be writing. If you have a favorite place and you are writing within the contemporary genre for your story, stick to what you know unless there's a reason for the plot to move elsewhere—unless you're feeling ambitious and want to take the time to research.

I use a foundation of what I know to craft stories quickly, and I write within contemporary genres so it works out great. If you must write outside of what you know, make sure you know the setting well. Don't put palm trees in southeast Idaho.

Here's a great way to figure out if you have the setting researched enough. Conduct this writing prompt: Have your character walk down the street. Just have them stroll through the town and admire the buildings, scenery, and businesses. It doesn't need to be in your story, but it'll help get your setting in your mind's eye. If you are struggling, go back to researching and then try the writing prompt again. Doing this in small increments of research and then writing will help you avoid the dreaded world-building syndrome many writers suffer from in their prewriting stages.

Research is great, but if you're not writing and only

researching, there is a problem.

CHAPTER 5
GOAL-SETTING FOR SUCCESS

THE FIRST THING YOU SHOULD know about success is

you're the only one who determines if you'll find it or not.

In this chapter, I want to go over some different key aspects

of success and what you, as a writer, can expect on your

road to getting there. Whether you want to write one book

or a hundred books, knowing what success looks like and

how to set yourself up for it is the key to achieving it.

FAILURE IS YOUR FRIEND

People fear failing more than anything else when they set out on a path worth traveling. This is true for all avenues in life. The problem with this is that failure is required in order to someday find success. Hitting points of failure mean you are learning what doesn't work on your journey. It's not the end, but just a turning point.

Before becoming a full-time writer and leaving my nine-to-five job, I had a decade of failures under my belt. I started companies that I had no business trying to start and I failed a ton. One time I tried to start a company that would deliver snack foods to people around the city. I never even got to the point in which I delivered a single snack. Many of my ideas and starts hit the pavement pretty quick while others lasted a while but still never took off because my heart wasn't in it. There was no passion or *why* other than to make more money and that wasn't enough for me.

My computer repair business start-up was called "My Tech" and I had that business operational for a while. I made business cards, handed out and hung up flyers, knocked on doors, and really pushed the business to succeed. I have a background in computers and I am really good at working on them, but there was really no passion behind it. So, I didn't succeed in the long run and the business was a total bust, but it still taught me that it was one more thing that didn't work for me, nor was it what I was destined to do. When I did start writing books, it wasn't an instant success either. It took months of failing and releasing horrible books to figure out what was good, what worked, and what didn't. It took almost two years to figure out what genre I was going to settle into and make my home. I failed constantly until I figured it out, and I still find myself failing at times. It's just part of moving up and growing. The best way to view failures is to see them as growing pains required for development in the areas of life we wish to improve. The only true failure is when you stop after failing.

SETTING A GOAL YOU CAN ACHIEVE

When you write down your goals, don't just write some fantasy goal that has no possibility of coming true. Stick to core goals that are very feasible and within your reach right now.

Example: Write a rough draft of XYZ manuscript within two months.

Change the time if needed, but you get the point. Your personal goals can work as deadlines for your writing projects. Often I find myself being lazy and procrastinating until the date approaches, so if you're like me you should try to make smaller goals that act more like deadlines. These will help launch you toward success.

I've met and read about a lot of authors who set daily word count goals. These smaller goals take you into the bigger ones. Some people set their goal at 1,000 words a day and for others, it's 2,000. You have to figure out how much time you can devote. There are plenty of authors out there who only can fit 250 words in a day, but as we have already learned in Chapter 3 Finding Time, at the end of the year that's over 91,000 words! Do what works for you and your life.

SETTING A GOAL YOU MIGHT ACHIEVE

Once you have set goals that are easily attainable for you, you can move into the more difficult goals. These are going to take a lot from you and will push you beyond what you could possibly do. They're still realistic, but they're just out of your grasp. If you can really buckle down and work on them, you can achieve them.

Example: Publish my book and earn over 100 reviews within the first 60 days.

Having a goal that's possible, but will require more effort out of you will automatically help condition your thoughts, decisions, and work habits to be geared toward achieving those high-reaching goals. Just writing it down on a sticky note and keeping it somewhere within eyesight will help you be more likely to hit that goal. You will naturally be drawn toward that goal and your mind will help you get there. It will still require purposeful steps on your part and a lot of hard work, but it's much easier when you let yourself know where you want to go.

SETTING A GOAL YOU DREAM OF ACHIEVING

The final piece of the puzzle for goal setting is setting one goal up for the entire year that you absolutely would *love* to achieve. It's most likely impossible, but it's still within the realm of reality. Making sure it's realistic will help keep it from being a ridiculous goal. Ridiculous goals are just a waste of time.

Example: Make $10,000 in a single month.

This goal isn't impossible for someone to achieve. It is

unlikely if you're starting out in the self-publishing industry, but it's not impossible. If you consider something like "a million dollars in one month," it would most likely be a waste of your time to think about. While it's possible, it resides outside of plausibility.

Giving yourself one, solid dream goal will help you set up for where you want to go in the long run. It's almost like a road map for your subconscious mind.

SECTION II: WRITING

CHAPTER 6
CREATING AN EXPERIENCE

READERS LOVE TO ESCAPE AND they do this through your story. You don't want to give them something they can't relate to or identify with, or they'll stop reading your book. You can't write about aliens that are nothing like humans, but you *can* write about aliens with human-like struggle (Hollywood example: Avatar). Make sure you make your characters relatable. The quicker you can build a connection to the reader, the better the experience for the reader.

This chapter will be going over the fundamentals of writing and creating a unique experience for your reader. You'll want to make sure you're not boring your readers at any point of the story, or you'll find readers setting down your book, oftentimes forgetting the fact that they were reading it.

IN THE BEGINNING . . .

The dreaded blinking cursor of doom lingers on a white word document, and you're pulling your hair out and cursing the day you were born. I've been there and it sucks. Luckily, there is hope.

First, what you should do in this situation is to open a fresh word document. Yes, I can hear you already ask, "What about the one that I have been working on?" My answer to that is still the same—a new document. Open that fresh document that doesn't contain any of that yucky feeling of utter doom that you had previously in front of you.

Now write. Write about your main character. View this not as the beginning of your novel, but instead as research. You need to get into your story, your character(s), and even your setting. If you read the point I made about setting and discovering where your story takes place, this is almost the exact same thing. Remember, this isn't your manuscript. This is to get the engine up and running. Once you're ready, switch back over to the other and dive in.

Another issue I've come across that you might encounter is you're partially into the beginning of the story and you know it's boring. If this is you, go ahead and remind yourself this is the first draft. Most likely, you'll be changing those first three to four chapters dramatically or maybe you'll even cut them out entirely. Many authors trash the first three chapters they write automatically to cut right into the story. It takes time to get into a story and find the voice that you are in search of—don't forget that.

CREATING SCENES

Scenes are what connect the story from one point to another point. They drive the story forward and keep things flowing. Each scene must advance the plot and drive the story further.

There's an important caveat that must be noted here about scenes: While you want the scenes to push the story forward, sometimes it's good to slow down and flesh out the setting, character, and the rest of the world that exists outside the storyline you're progressing.

Be sure to have a flowing story, but allow yourself to slow down. It's all about pacing. One thing after another makes for a fast-paced novel, but often this can take away from the experience. The slower scenes are opportunities to let your character's emotions, life, and motivations flourish and help enrich the experience for the reader. Pay close attention to your story's pace and allow the slow scenes to creep in once in a while.

SCENES: SHOWING UP LATE & LEAVING EARLY

Showing up late and leaving early is probably not the best practice with your friends and family, but it's vital for gripping scenes. The scenes you craft need to be full of purpose and rich with driving points to move forward in the story. Nobody wants to read about two talking heads greeting each other and exchanging hellos with nothing going on. Get to the point quickly and get out quickly. There's nothing more boring than reading a scene in which basic dialogue is exchanged and the reader is forced to listen to standard greetings they themselves encounter every day.

Example:

"Hi," Tim said to Sally.

"Hello," she replied.

"How are you?" he asked.

"Good," she replied.

When you go through your revisions (we'll talk more about

this later in the book), you'll want to make sure you tighten up dialogue and scenes so there is a purpose with each sentence and paragraph within the manuscript.

WRITING DIALOGUE

Dialogue is an art form and even the most experienced writers struggle with it. Keeping a conversation flowing in a story is much more difficult than it is made to look by the prolific writers of today. The tendency most writers have is to expose plot within dialogue, and it's a bad practice. Let's take a look at an example below.

Example: "Hey, Sally. Did you see that wreck on Monroe on your way home from work?"

Nodding, she replied, "Yeah. I noticed the blue Honda Accord had white paint on the side where it was hit by a Toyota Prius. Wonder if Jeff Krunk hit it?"

The above example is pretty bad. If the author needs to

work in details of the car, they should be using the story to do it, not forcing it through dry dialogue scenes. An example of what the author could do is to have the guy who speaks the first line have actually seen Sally at the scene (her car) and mention it in their conversation. Working in details of what you want the reader to know is important. Many times, you'll find yourself adding hints, clues, or other information throughout the story in the revision stages. Another important thing to know about dialogue is the subtext: not what's said, but how it's being said.

Wrong:

"I love you," Sally said.

"I love you too," Brad replied.

Better:

"I love you." Tears streamed down her cheeks and her heart pounded as she waited for Brad's response.

Brad hesitated. His eyes held the hurt from the past as they welled with tears, but he was able to push it aside for love and broke into a smile. "I love you, too."

Dialogue can be difficult, and you'll find many writers will spend time in coffee shops and out in public with a notebook and pen just so they can study the art of conversation. There's a fine line between sounding realistic and just forcing your characters to push the plot forward. Be careful and always refine your dialogue on the revision part of your writing.

ENGAGING DIALOGUE

One of the most important things to avoid when crafting dialogue is the dreaded talking heads. Back and forth is sometimes okay and completely reasonable; other times the reader can become tired and bored, often losing track of who is talking. When a reader has to look up to see who is saying what, you're not doing it correctly. All the white space can give them a headache as well, so be sure to keep the people moving and doing something while they're talking. Let's take a look at a few examples.

Example (Boring Dialogue):

Heading into the kitchen, I found Micah doing the dishes. I smiled as I patted him on the shoulder and asked, "Want some help with those?"

"Sure. Glad to have you back, Taylor. This place hasn't been the same without you keeping everyone in line. Sherwood tries to keep an eye on the guys, but everyone knows you're the one that keeps the order around here."

"Good to be back. I did some more reading in my Bible last night and talked to Megan a little bit."

"That's great to hear!"

Example (Engaging Dialogue):

Heading into the kitchen, I found Micah doing the dishes. I smiled as I patted him on the shoulder and asked, "Want some help with those?"

"Sure," he said as he gave me the towel that was draped over his shoulder. "Glad to have you back, Taylor. This place hasn't been the same without you keeping everyone in line. Sherwood tries to keep an eye on the guys, but everyone knows you're the one that keeps the order around here."

"Good to be back." I grabbed a plate from the second sink and dried it. "I did some more reading in my Bible last night and talked to Megan a little bit."

Stopping from washing the plate he had in his hand, Micah said, "That's great to hear!"

The above dialogue with engagement helps the reader not only keep track of who is talking; it keeps them in the story and scene that is occurring. While washing dishes isn't a big deal when it comes to the plot, it does help keep the dialogue separated and highlights Micah's character of being a God-serving man. Also, when Micah stopped washing the plate and directed his attention to Cole, it really showed how much he cared about Cole and their relationship. This type of scene building works on multiple layers and helps enrich the reading experience.

CHAPTER 7
WHEN & WHERE TO WRITE

WRITING THE STORY YOU WISH to write is going to take an incredible amount of time and concentration. It's important that you not only find the time to write your story but to stay consistent with your writing. Don't confuse this chapter with *finding time*, which is just finding the time in life to dedicate to writing. This is different. This is about when and where to do your writing.

WHEN TO CRAFT YOUR MASTERPIECE

Mornings will forever be my best time to write. I can
continue writing through the day, but the morning is when
I'm at my peak, personally. It's good to try all different times
of the day and record the results. There are a few people I
know who love to write at night and craft their stories when
everyone is heading to bed. It's about finding what works
for you. Some people have to find pockets of time in the
day.

Finding your own perfect writing time can be difficult with
the demands of your job, family, and everything else, but I
want to direct you back to Chapter 3 Finding Time if that's
an issue. There's always a reason why you can't, but the
truth is we always find time for the things we want to do.

WHERE TO CRAFT YOUR MASTERPIECE

This is one of the most important pieces to your success as a
writer, in my opinion. Having a place where you can focus
and disappear into a different world is required for writing

fiction. It's not something that is recommended, it's vital.

The reason why it's so important is because you, as a writer, are basically vanishing into another world. The act of writing is done through your subconscious. Through the unseen. You are traveling the seas, taking wormholes to other universes, or going back in time. If you're yelling at kids while you're writing a story, that story is going to suffer. Kids down for a nap? Take an opportunity to write. Free time while the family is reading and doing homework? Take the opportunity to write.

Find that place and time you can disappear. This might play into your availability and time allotment. If you're unable to step away from life and have quietness behind a closed door, you might need to dig a little deeper into finding time. Coffee shops are not recommended for writing unless you can pop on the headphones and hop on your broomstick to your fantasy world. If you do travel to public areas to craft your masterpiece, make sure it works for you and you have the time to sink into your writing. In my own experience, it's been a waste. I spend an hour getting showered, packed, and down to the coffee shop, just to find myself constantly distracted by other people around me. Even with headphones on, I'm drawn to listen in on others and engage with the world around me.

Wherever you choose to write, make sure it's consistent. When I walk into my writing room—my bedroom—I flip on the lamp in the corner and it's almost as if it activates a switch in my mind. I'm transported to a new world and I'm able to sit down and write.

CHAPTER 8
FURST DRAFFS SUK

THE MOST IMPORTANT CHAPTER IN this book is this

one. New writers struggle with *not* editing their work over

and over again. It's pure insanity to do this, but it's part of

being new. I'm guilty of doing this in the beginning, but I've

gotten better about it. I'd re-read what I wrote the day

before, or worse, I'd re-read everything I wrote up until

where I left off last and edit every part of the writing. This is

an utter waste of time!

3

The first draft is where you get the story down on paper (or screen). I approach a first draft by getting the structure and idea I want onto the pages. I need to know what I'm working with to develop the story in the revisions. Getting that story down quickly is crucial. Let's go over a few different things to keep in mind when you're writing your first draft.

NEVER EDIT YOUR FIRST DRAFT

Everyone is tempted to edit their work whenever they re-read it. It's a natural thing to do when you're writing. I can't read a single piece of my writing without wanting to edit it. Be sure not to get into a routine of self-editing. Minor tweaks are okay but don't get stuck in the nasty habit of going over everything before you continue writing.

Your goal in the first draft, like I said before and I can't say enough, is to get the story down. Form the idea in its entirety. Don't worry about fancy and pretty sentences; they'll change. You can add all the prettiness in your revision stages later.

TAKE LOTS OF NOTES

Since you won't be editing and fixing your work as you go through, it's a good idea to take lots and lots of notes. I like to keep a running tab of important notes on each chapter so I can later read them to get a feel for the story when I need a refresher, or go to write the next time. This also eliminates the temptation to edit what I have already written because I can get back into the story without actually reading the manuscript.

Another great thing about notes is foreshadowing. You can add things you should probably mention earlier in the book so in the next revision, you can add it. I like to highlight and color code different types of notes (not all, just some—like foreshadowing). Foreshadowing is always red when it's critical. Green means it can be mentioned earlier or it's something to keep in mind. Little tricks like these can help revisions become less painful. The less painful the revisions are, the happier you'll be.

The only time I use the actual manuscript to look back during the first draft is when I need to verify something that was said, or a name, or something similar that was not included in the notes. It rarely happens, but it does happen sometimes.

CHAPTER 9
REVISE, CRY, REVISE

THERE IS ONLY ONE PART of writing that I loathe—the

revisions. It's not merely the second draft of the story, it's

far beyond that. It's the third, fourth, and fifth revision of a

manuscript where you just want to gouge your eyeballs out.

I know that seems intense, but it's really mild in comparison

to how it feels to read the same thing over and over again

until you can't seem to see anything else wrong with it. It's

literally mind numbing.

The entire writing process itself is quite an emotional rollercoaster. Often, you'll find yourself bouncing between thinking you're a genius and thinking you shouldn't ever be allowed to write another word.

This type of behavior is found in only two types of people—the mentally insane and those who write stories. If you aren't there, don't worry. You'll get there someday.

Revising is a brutal part of the writing process, but it also comes with a lot of fun. There are times in which I read something I wrote and wonder who did it because it was quite brilliant to be anything of mine. Then, other times, I wonder who wrote it because it is utter trash.

The most annoying part of revisions is the fact that they don't even catch every problem you have in the manuscript. Many times your eyes will trick you into thinking something is written in a certain way, but in reality, it's not. That's why it's crucial to have beta readers, proofreaders, line editors, and so on. I cover that in Chapter 10 Fine-Tuning the Manuscript.

FIRST REVISIONS

Go through your story and use your notes to fix what you
already know needs fixing. Don't worry about actually
reading the story from start to finish on this first pass-
through. It's a waste of time (notice how I mention this a lot
in the book? I find many things to be time wasters and with
a life outside of writing, these have to be avoided). Instead,
focus on the major areas where you took notes.

There will be specific notes you aren't sure need to be
incorporated into your story; save those for your actual
read-through. This first revision is only for the major fixes
and foreshadowing.

SECOND REVISION

Read through your story and fine-tune every sentence you
come across. This is when the magic really begins to flow
into the story. Spend time crafting each sentence to flow
smoothly, and bring the world and story to life. Some
people will naturally write plenty of description and

beautiful prose in the first draft. If you're anything like me, you'll be working on making your work shine in the second set of revisions and each set of revisions beyond.

CHAPTER 10
FINE-TUNING THE MANUSCRIPT

WHEN YOU HAVE YOUR MANUSCRIPT where you are

happy with it, you'll come to the point where you need to

send it to someone who can tear it apart. Sounds fun, right?

It's not too bad, and it gives you a break from the

manuscript. The next time you come back to it, your eyes

have had a chance to heal. There are a few different ways to

get a manuscript edited. Some cost you thousands of

dollars, others are free, and the rest fall somewhere between those two extremes. In this chapter, I will cover each area of editing that you should be aware of and explain how to proceed through each one.

DEVELOPMENTAL EDITING

You love your manuscript and think it's amazing at this point. Now it's time for fresh eyes that can help you shape the story (where it needs it) and point out the plot holes. There are professional developmental editors that can cost you thousands, but there are also more affordable ways of development editing. If you want to pay top dollar, go hunt one down that specializes in your genre and go for it. If you're broke or can't afford that kind of thing, keep reading. First, let's take a moment to discuss what developmental editing is and is not. Developmental editing is when someone takes your story and finds all the problems with it regarding the storyline. They look for loose ends and incorrect information (example: historical inaccuracies). They help you shape characters and rip out entire scenes that are useless. They won't fine-tune your grammar or word choice most of the time, but instead they look at the structural integrity of the manuscript. They can be ruthless, but these people can help make a good manuscript great. Now let's talk about finding someone who can fit this role without breaking the bank. This is going to be someone who is either willing to work with you for a profit on their part (this is what I did) or it's going to be someone who just loves your genre. Whatever you do, it's important you find the right fit. If it doesn't feel right in the sample edit (most editors will edit a portion of your work), go with your gut. The last thing you want to do is send a manuscript to your "developmental editor" only to get it back with a thumbs up and an "I loved it." These people aren't helping you. They might be sweet and really nice, but they're not being helpful.

You need someone to shred your work into pieces so you can put it back together and make it pretty again. I will warn you—if you haven't ever written anything and you're trying to find someone who fits this role, it's going to be hard. In my early days, I had to skip the developmental editor and just find beta readers who could report back issues they found. If you do that, make sure you let them know to spot any plot holes or issues throughout their reading and make them feel valuable. Spouses and family members aren't recommended because they tend to be biased toward your work, but if it's required (because you can't find anyone else), make sure you press the importance of how ruthless they can and should be. Try to still steer clear of them if possible.

Once you take the manuscript to the slaughterhouse, start fixing the problems (that you agree are issues) and begin revisions again. If you go the route of multiple beta readers, be sure to recognize the patterns where they reveal what they say is wrong.

BETA READERS

Beta readers will comprise loyal fans of your work or those

you find willing to give your piece a shot. You can find some on Goodreads.com and a few Facebook groups, but don't be discouraged if you receive a low amount of replies in your hunt. Also, don't become discouraged when even a smaller percent actually beta read and provide feedback. It's just part of the process. Always request more than you want. If you desire five beta readers' feedback, you better be sending out at least fifteen to twenty copies.

Beta readers are going to help you fine-tune your manuscript and they'll pick out a multitude of issues depending on who's reading. But, some of them won't. The help can come in a multitude of ways: commas, sentence structure, plots, sub-plots, etc. . . . It really comes down to the one reading and what they're willing to spot.

LINE EDITOR

Once you're satisfied with your revisions, it's time to find a line editor. This part is crucial in order to present a polished and final book. The line editor will take care of a lot of the grammar and sentence structure issues.

While you will need to invest money in a line editor, there's good news. As I mentioned earlier, most line editors will provide a free sample of their work. You send them a portion of your manuscript and they'll edit it for free to show you how well they do so. This is a great way to test someone out to see if they're a good fit for you.

It took me half-dozen editors before I found one that prevented bad reviews from coming in. It's hard work to find a decently-priced editor, but when you put in the research and time in finding a high-quality one, your readers will thank you (in the form of not leaving bad reviews).

A few editors will even break up the cost in payments, which can help tremendously if you're on a tight budget.

Getting a quality line editor is essential and if you need help finding one, head over to a website such as www.kboards.com, as well as the Writer's Café (it's located under the "Author" menu item along the top). There you can do a search for editors and browse the yellow pages

thread inside the Writer's Café.

Try multiple editors, get price quotes, and compare their

styles of work.

When you do get the work back from the editor, carefully

go over every change and make sure you're okay with the

changes. You don't want to auto-accept everything. There

might be parts you found crucial to your story and would

rather not change. A great example of this would be

dialogue in which the person speaks more formally, but the

editor changed all the instances of "should not" to

"shouldn't" and messed up the voice.

Pro-Tip: Take it to the next level and do a full read of
your manuscript aloud after your line editor is done.
Even editors will often miss a few here and there.

PROOFREADERS

You're getting close to publication and you should pat yourself on the back for that fact alone. You've done a lot up until this point and now it's time to gather a few more readers who can conduct a read-through on your story. While many companies that provide line edits will offer proofreading, it's often more affordable to ask people to proofread (they'll recommend fixing minor issues if you ask them to). I usually ask people to keep an eye out for typos or missing words. At this stage, your manuscript should be so polished it only has maybe one or two issues.

Facebook groups, fans, and Goodreads are all great places to find proofreaders. If you need to hire someone to proofread (professional proofreaders will catch more) ask your editor if they have recommendations.

SECTION III: PUBLISHING

CHAPTER 11
FORMATTING

TAKE A BREATH AND RELAX for a minute if you're on this chapter to learn how to format. This means you have not only written a manuscript, you've revised it A LOT and you've already shared the manuscript with multiple people—which is quite the nerve-wracking accomplishment. I'm sure you're excited to be this close to publication. It's quite a feat! Good job!

The reason I tell you to take a break is because the formatting section needs your full attention. You need to be a hundred percent involved if you're going to do this right. Bad formatting is one thing that can throw your sales in the toilet. If the reader has a bad experience upon just opening your book, you're in *big* trouble. Luckily, if you read and apply the information in this chapter, your readers are going to be thankful. If you want to skip a lot of these sections, you can simply use the template I have available at benjaminchapin.com/writing-tools/ under *Formatting Resources*. If you do it that way, you'll be able to simply copy and paste your manuscript into the file and replace my info and words with yours. This template shows you what the inside of all my books look like. I just simply change it for each new book I write. The template already has all the correct formatting done for you; however, in this chapter, I will explain how I did the formatting. I will also provide some tips, as well as do's and don'ts, so be sure not to entirely skip over it if you choose to go with the template.

For the actual software side of formatting, I use Microsoft Word, and that's the program I'll discuss primarily. There are many programs available out there that are designed for laying out pages and are e-book/paperback friendly. If you own one of those, such as Adobe's InDesign, I'd suggest looking up formatting tips and tricks through YouTube or Google, as it is not covered in this book.

FRONT AND BACK MATTER

The front and back matter are the first and last parts of the book. It's what the reader sees first when they open your book and the last thing they'll see when they're done. It's where you find the title, book legalities, and all that "extra" stuff that isn't the story. You have an opportunity to maximize these areas for a huge impact on the reader. Don't neglect them.

For the front matter, you'll need the Title Page, Copyright information page, Dedication (if applicable), and Table of Contents.

For the back matter, you'll want a sneak peek page (gives the reader a taste of the next in the series or another piece of your work), Resource/Offer page (deals or freebies that entice the reader to subscribe to your mailing list), other books page, author page, and a note page (requests that the reader leaves a review).

TABLE OF CONTENTS

The table of contents is the menu for your reader. It'll make it so they can jump to different chapters and all your back matter. Don't forget this part. It's crucial that they are able to navigate your book, and the Table of Contents provides that ability.

The template will already have all the settings you need for your Table of Contents. After you get your book into the book template, just right-click and select "update" on the Table of Contents.

I made my table of contents in the template by following the directions below.

1.) Highlight each chapter heading and change it to "Heading 1" at the top of the Word document. Go through the entirety of the manuscript and make this change for each chapter. Once that's done, go to your back matter and make sure all headings match the "Heading 1" style.

2.) Insert a blank page between the dedication (if you have one) and the beginning of your story (Prologue or Chapter 1).

3.) On the blank page, type "Table of Contents" at the top of the page and then hit Enter.

4.) Go to References (top of screen across the top in the tabs) -> Table of Contents and click "Insert Table of Contents . . ."

5.) Uncheck the "page number" option and change levels to 1. After customizing the look of it, click okay and your table of contents will be generated.

6.) Test the table of contents out by holding control and clicking on them one at a time.

MICROSOFT WORD

There are a few things that will make your life much easier. The first thing you want to do is turn on the "Show formatting marks" (See Figure 11.1). Making these marks visible will be annoying at first, but after you get used to it, it'll save your hide when it comes to converting your book from Word document to e-book format (more on that process later). This allows you to see all formatting and you'll be able to catch those nasty mistakes (extra spaces, tabbed paragraphs, etc. . . .).

Figure 11.1 Formatting Marks

You can access the options for paragraphs through the little menu arrow option for "Paragraph" in Microsoft Word (see Figure 11.2 below).

Figure 11.2 *Paragraph Options*

The next thing you'll want to do is make sure the beginning of each paragraph has an indent of 0.01" (see Figure 11.3 below).

Figure 11.3 Indentation – First Line

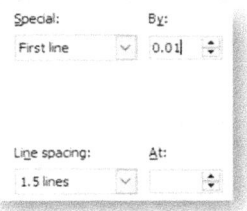

Each paragraph following the first one should have an indent of 0.50" until the end of the chapter. Also, change the line spacing to 1.5 (see Figure 11.4) for the entire document.

Figure 11.4 Indentation – Following Paragraphs

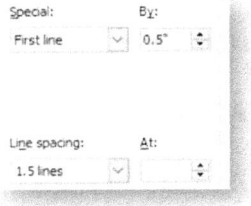

If you're looking to add more chapters using the template, simply follow these directions:

1.) Select Chapter 1 heading and highlight all the way through the filler text.

2.) Right click, then "copy."

3.) Click "Insert" tab in Microsoft Word -> Click "Page Break."

4.) Right click, then "paste."

MICROSOFT WORD: PAGE LAYOUT

The page size is not relevant—A4 or letter is fine. You do not need to consider margins, just use the standard settings.

MICROSOFT WORD: MANUSCRIPT FORMATTING

- Separate chapters with a page break between chapters. You can find the page break command in the "Insert" tab on the top ribbon in Microsoft Word.

- Separate paragraphs with a single paragraph break (just hit the enter key once). Do not use double paragraph breaks (too much white space and will annoy readers).

- Do not use tabs or multiple spaces.

- Use a standard font like Times New Roman.

- 12pt font for main body.

- Use only black text.

MICROSOFT WORD: QUICK STYLES AND OTHER MISC.

- IDEALLY, use the "Normal" Quick Style in Word for the main body of your manuscript, and manage the appearances of your body text through the Quick Styles options.

- If you need to make certain words or sentences stand out, try to use only basic formatting found in your menu such as **bold**, *italic*, or have some fun and use ALL-CAPS.

- Use the Heading styles available in the Quick Style list. Heading 1 for chapter titles, Heading 2 for subtitles or section headings, etc. If you want to customize these to look different, make sure to research on Google what's acceptable for books.

MICROSOFT WORD: IMAGES

Images are easily inserted into your e-book. Make sure it's inserted on its own line (you can insert an image through the insert tab in Word). Resize accordingly.

MICROSOFT WORD: LINKS

Use the hyperlink menu option in Word under the "Insert" tab found along the ribbon up top.

MICROSOFT WORD: DON'TS OF FORMATTING

- *Don't* add page numbers (e-book version)
- *Don't* add headers and footers
- *Don't* add borders, background colors, or background images
- *Don't* add fancy drop caps at the start of each chapter
- *Don't* add different color text

- *Don't* add multi-column layouts

- *Don't* add text boxes

CONVERTING TO PDF, MOBI, AND EPUB

To format into various formats (PDF, MOBI, and EPUB) you can use the website www.Draft2Digital.com or my personal favorite—Calibre. First, we'll discuss Draft2Digital.com.

Draft2Digital:

1.) Sign up at www.Draft2Digital.com, log in, and click "Add Book."

2.) Follow directions and upload book file (Word document).

3.) Once on the proof stage of the process, you can download the format you wish (just don't proceed if you don't want to publish the book). See issues with the result produced? Go back and make tweaks to the

Word document, then go back to the step where you add the book file again.

Calibre is software you can find for free at www.calibre-ebook.com.This software has a bit of a learning curve to it; but once you get used to it, it's an amazing tool and highly useful. You can output to PDF, MOBI, and EPUB (among others if your heart so desires). Watch this full tutorial over at YouTube through this link https://youtu.be/44alkLGlMNQ. Otherwise, the directions are as follows.

1.) Download the software from www.calibre-ebook.com and install it.

2.) Click "Add Book" and select your book file.

Figure 11.5 Calibre – Add Books

3.) Click "Edit Metadata."

Figure 11.6 Calibre – Edit Metadata

4.) Fill out the details. Save and close window.

Figure 11.7 Calibre ~ Metadata Options

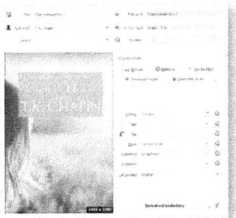

5.) Click "Convert Books."

Figure 11.8 Calibre – Convert

6.) Select the format you desire it to convert into (PDF,

MOBI, or EPUB).

Figure 11.9 Calibre – Output Format Selection

7.) Go through options. Most can be left as is. If you have issues with the output, you can return to these options and make tweaks as needed (otherwise refer to your Word document to fix the issues). Click "OK" when satisfied to start conversion.

8.) Wait for the job to finish.

Figure 11.10 Calibre – Jobs

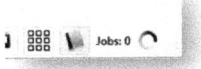

9.) Right click on the main window in Calibre where your book is and select "Open Containing Folder" (all converted files for the book will appear in that folder. Move them to a more permanent location when you're happy).

Figure 11.11 Calibre – Containing Folder

If you don't want to mess with any of this stuff, you can always hire someone on a place like www.Fiverr.com to do all the converting for you. Creating these files is going to come in handy when you go to hand out ARCs (Advance Reading Copies) and Review Copies.

PAPERBACKS

To format a Paperback, you can use a multitude of different services. I'll recommend using www.createspace.com. It doesn't cost anything to publish a paperback with this company, and they're easy to work with since they're partnered with Amazon.

You can find templates for interior designing (and no, I do not mean for your house!). Visit https://forums.createspace.com/en/community/docs/DOC-1323 and download the corresponding size you need. If you need help or wish to have design incorporated, I'd suggest looking at www.Fiverr.com for an interior book designer, or you can research issues online that you are running into.

CHAPTER 12
BOOK COVERS

DESIGNING YOUR OWN BOOK COVER can risk your product looking unprofessional. I've been using programs like Photoshop for over a decade and this was one shortcut I was able to tap into. If you have any kind of experience with Photoshop or other programs, I'd suggest creating your own book cover as long as it looks as professional as the ones you'll find in the top 10 charts. Otherwise, you'll be paying anywhere from $5 to $2,000 per cover. There is also www.canva.com, which is great since it only costs $1 for most Kindle cover options, but you do risk looking like the others who use it. The other option is having me design your cover. If you'd like me to design your book cover, I charge a modest fee and you can order a book cover at benjaminchapin.com/book-covers/.

SIZES

E-book – 3200 x 4800 pixels (standard)

Paperback – Varies depending on size of book. After you've made your paperback interior (covered in the formatting section), go to www.createspace.com/Help/Book/Artwork.do and fill in the requested information (pages, trim size, etc. . . .). The website will generate a PDF file for you to download, which can be imported into your design program. The file will show you the margins that you need to create the paperback layout (front and back).

DO-IT-YOURSELF COVERS

If you decide to make your own book cover, I've collected a few different resources that should be able to help you on your journey. While these tutorials are very basic in nature, they should provide you with enough information to get you started.

Canva.com – https://youtu.be/ujX9-slHquw

Gimp – https://youtu.be/dFDKj4LKOmc

Microsoft Word – https://youtu.be/h_6zDyBZ9Mw

Photoshop - https://youtu.be/PTfos2WBOmw

Illustrator – https://youtu.be/niqtP4rQflM

Make sure you have a clear understanding of how colors work and what colors complement each other (See Figure

12.1 below). You can also view a larger color wheel at

benjaminchapin.com/writing-tools/.

Figure 12.1 – Color Wheel

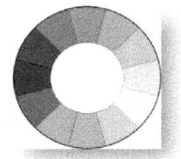

PICTURES FOR YOUR COVERS

Do not use pictures on Google images for your

cover design. This is illegal. You need to find images

that are for commercial use. There are free repositories

out there along with paid options. Each website has

legal documentation you can and should read. I'm

providing you with a collection of different resources

that are cheap or free. I will warn you, if you do find

pictures on these sites, especially the free ones, you'll

risk seeing your images on another person's cover, so

be careful. If you know pretty couples or what you

want on a cover, borrow someone's camera and see if they'll be willing to be on a book cover. There's absolutely no chance of someone having the same cover if you do it this way.

Free and Low-Cost Photo Repositories:

Pixabay.com – Free images

Freeimages.com - Free images

Dollarphotoclub.com – Bargain Images

Fotolia.com – Bargain Images

123rf.com – Bargain Images

If you're still in need of that perfect photo, just keep hunting and be sure to check the license information out on each picture and website so you can make sure you're not breaking the law.

INSPIRATION FOR COVERS

When creating your cover, you need to make sure it fits into your genre of writing. You can find inspiration by browsing the best seller lists on Amazon for similar books to get a good idea of the direction you should go. What I like to do is look at the best sellers, incorporate *some* of the same aspects, but also bring my own taste to it so I stand out in a good way.

Make sure you don't skimp on book covers. The famous saying states not to judge a book by the cover, but consumers do.

CHAPTER 13
HOW TO PUBLISH THE BOOK

HOW AMAZING DOES IT FEEL TO have your book ready

to publish? Okay, okay. We'll get on with this chapter.

AMAZON KDP

If you have ever shopped at Amazon, you already have an

Amazon account and you'll be able to use that throughout

the process of publishing. Be sure to use the same e-mail

address *everywhere* you do author-related stuff. It'll keep your mind from exploding. If you need to sign up for an Amazon account, I'd recommend heading over to kdp.amazon.com and clicking "Sign Up." If you plan to make a new e-mail address only used for your author account, I'd recommend Gmail. You can sign up at accounts.google.com/SignUp.

A complete how-to guide on publishing through KDP is located on YouTube if you would prefer a video over reading. You can find that video at youtu.be/A29PWJdGSyo. Before you get started on publishing your book, you should first set up an author profile at Amazon's Author Central. I'll walk you through that process now.

1.) Go to authorcentral.amazon.com

2.) Click "Join Now" and get signed up.

3.) Be sure to use the author name you'll use for your books (You'll be returning to Author Central to claim your books later).

4.) Upload a photo of yourself, write a bio (use other similar authors' bios for inspiration), and fill everything out you desire. Submit the changes and you're ready to go.

Once you have finished setting up your profile in Author Central, it'll be time for you to get that book uploaded to Amazon.

1.) Go to kdp.amazon.com

2.) Sign in and link the account you used at Author Central (good to stay consistent).

3.) On the Bookshelf tab, select "Create New Title."

4.) Select at the top if you wish to be in the KDP Select Program.

a. This makes your book exclusively sold at Amazon. It also includes:

i. Free promo days or Kindle Countdown Days (Read More in the Marketing Section on Amazon Promotions).

ii. Kindle Unlimited & Prime Memberships have the ability to loan your book (Read More in the Marketing Section on Amazon Promotions).

5.) Fill in the required information (Title, Subtitle, Keywords etc. . . .). Check out the Marketing Section and the Product Page Optimization for help with title, keywords, and so on.

6.) Upload your book cover & your interior book file (fully formatted).

7.) Click the preview option and view your book on multiple formats to see if there are any issues you might have missed (don't skip this).

8.) Go to the next page and set the price (Amazon provides a free tool that will recommend a price OR you can use your own research, which is covered in the Marketing Section of this book in Chapter 16 Page Optimization).

9.) Click Publish! Try not to freak out too much . . . well, actually, go ahead and freak out. You did it! Congratulations! Now wait for your book to publish, which can take up to 48 hours, but usually shows up as a page within a few hours.

AMAZON REPORTS

To view your sales report dashboard, head over to kdp.amazon.com/reports. Sign into your author account for Amazon. Here you can track all your sales, pre-orders, previous month's sales, and so on. It's the hub for your Amazon author profile.

DRAFT2DIGITAL (APPLE, BARNES & NOBLE, AND BEYOND)

Draft2Digital is a company that will distribute your book to multiple retailers and take a cut off the top of your profits for themselves. Right now, they publish to iBooks, Nook (Barnes & Noble), Kobo, Oyster, Page Foundry, Scribd, and Tolino. Even with all those retailers, I personally don't see enough sales to justify not being exclusive to Amazon. The biggest loss I've experienced from going wide ("wide" is the lingo used to describe publishing to multiple platforms) is losing the loans and/or page reads (perk of being in Kindle Unlimited and exclusive with Amazon). The page reads I receive from publishing exclusively with Amazon far outweigh the sales I see with the other retailers. While this will most likely change at some point, I wouldn't recommend going wide in the beginning of your writing career. Keep it simple as you dip your toes into the publishing world.

That said, I will give you some information about publishing with Draft2Digital.com since I've published and have some books currently published with them that are not exclusive with Amazon. I want to go ahead and say this one more time because it's important. Your book cannot be exclusive to Amazon (in the KDP Select Program) *and* be published on multiple platforms. It's on a per-book basis, not per author.

If you decide to go wide, keep a file separate for "other" vendors outside of Amazon. Places like iBooks will reject your book if you have links going to competitors.

How to upload on Draft2Digital:

1. Go to www.draft2digital.com

2. Sign up for an account.

3. Click "Add New Book" at the top of the screen inside the dashboard,

4. Upload your book file (make sure there are no links to Amazon inside the file).

5. Fill out the information requested.

6. Upload book cover.

    Continue through screens and quality check the files produced. If issues are present, fix the Word document and re-upload.

CREATESPACE PAPERBACK

Createspace.com is a great way to publish your paperback without hurting your wallet. It doesn't matter if you're exclusive with Amazon or not, you can always publish a paperback version. Plus, it's free and easy. Having a paperback copy of your book is a bit of a pain with the formatting and cover, but it'll look great to have one and increase your credibility to readers. CreateSpace is a printon-demand sister company to Amazon.

<u>Here's how to get started:</u>

1. Sign up for an account at www.createspace.com

2. Once you are at the Member Dashboard, select "New Title."

3. Note the FREE CreateSpace assigned ISBN-13 and the ISBN-10. You'll want to update your interior book file you formatted with these numbers.

4. Upload interior book file and verify no errors are appearing in the proof.

5. Upload the book cover and submit the files for review.

Please note: It can take up to 24 hours for approval and up to seven days for it to appear on Amazon. If you do not see the book linked on Amazon, contact Amazon KDP Support (kdp.amazon.com) and let them know about the issue. They'll link the paperback and the e-book for you manually.

AUDIOBOOKS ON ACX

ACX.com is a sister company of Amazon (I know, big surprise, eh?). Also, this doesn't impede on your exclusiveness with Amazon. This is an avenue to build your credibility and your flexibility with your readers. Giving your readers an alternative way to consume your product with little effort on your part is always a good idea. It's important to note that audiobooks are gaining popularity. Whether it's on the morning commute, working out at the gym or just out running errands, people are listening more and more.

With audiobooks, you, the author, have already done the bulk of the work. You've written it and already have it published in e-book. Now you just need someone to transform that into a polished audiobook. It's a smart move to maximize your book's income streams.

Here's how to get started with Audiobooks:

1. Head over to www.acx.com

2. Log into the site using your Amazon credentials.

3. Click "Add Your Title" on the top right of the screen once you're logged in.

4. Fill out all the required information.

5. If you're going the least expensive route, select the "Royalty Split" option when you arrive at it. The other option allows you to pay someone per finished hour of audio recording. This price usually ranges between $100 and $1000 and most novels run anywhere between 4 hours all the way up to 13 hours.

6. Once happy, post to ACX.

7. Start searching for narrators on the site and send them messages requesting they audition and letting them know the closing date of auditions.

If you desire to record your own audiobook and have the time to invest along with the equipment, that's an option and will net you a considerably larger amount of the royalties. I don't recommend this unless you have a nice voice, nice equipment, and a good deal of time on your hands. If you have a bestselling book that seems to be doing well on Amazon, ACX.com will (sometimes) pick it up for what's called a stipend. This stipend will pay the narrator $100 per finished hour and also will give them a royalty share. It's absolutely insane how many auditions you get once you have one of those "stipend" stickers attached to a title. The stipend will give you more auditions to listen to and, in turn, help you find a narrator who is perfect for the job.

SECTION IV: MARKETING LIKE A BOSS

CHAPTER 14
NOW GIVE IT AWAY

ALL THIS HARD WORK YOU'VE been doing is now going to be given away for free. What? Free? That's right. This is especially important in your early days when your name is just a name in the sea of millions. You'll want to give it away to anyone and everyone that you come in contact with who will read it. I'll give you a moment to process that.

You okay?

Good.

Now give it away! I wouldn't recommend pitching your gritty fantasy novel to a clean romance reader, but anyone interested in a book like yours should get a free copy for a review. Get your book to as many readers as you can before you publish. The longer you can wait to publish, the bigger impact you can have due to the readers ready to publish their reviews on release day.

ADVANCE READING COPIES (ARCs)

Don't believe anyone who tells you that you shouldn't give your book away to people. Go check their sales ranks on Amazon and see how well they are doing. There are three reasons why someone would say something like this. One, they don't make any money and refuse to give their work away for free. Two, they've been writing and publishing for a long time and started when there wasn't as much competition. Three, they give stuff away but view you as a threat and don't want you to succeed. When people who don't write or publish in any capacity tell you it's a bad idea, just smile and nod. Most of your friends and especially your family will think this technique is insane, but they'll lose their minds entirely with other parts of what you do. Ignore them. Even the Big 5 publishing companies give books away for free when it comes to review copies.

Make sure you've done the blurb writing for your book already. If you haven't, go check out Chapter 16 Page Optimization. It's vital to have a blurb before you start asking people if they want to read your book. Otherwise, they'll ask what your book is about and you'll say, "Umm . . . There're these guys that do things and it's really cool." Or, "Have you ever read XYZ? It's a cross between that and ABC. It's really good." Don't be that person. Get the blurb done.

What you want to do first is head over to www.goodreads.com/author/how_to. Learn about the author program and get your author profile set up (use the same photo and author blurb you used from the book and the author central account—be consistent). After you do that, it's time to hunt.

Join all the groups you can think of joining that are related to your genre. Christian books, fantasy readers . . . whatever it is, get connected and plugged in. If you can start this long before the book comes out and really communicate with others in the group, they'll be more eager to read your book(s).

1. Post an excerpt from your book in groups that allow it and ask for people interested in reading it to contact you.

2. For those who reply to the thread, send a private message, or e-mail you, ask them what format they want (see formatting chapter for how to convert to PDF, MOBI, and EPUB).

3. E-mail anybody a copy of the book (send a format they want). Also, put the title of your book in the subject line. Something like "Book Title – ARC

Copy" or "Book Title – Review Copy." Doing this will make it easier when you come back around to follow up with people to see if they've read it and remind them of the release or upcoming release day.

4. Keep looking for those who could be interested in a copy of your book.

Please note: Make sure you are asking for honest reviews, not good reviews. Asking for good reviews is dishonest and goes against the rules of ethics.

Now head over to Facebook and join author and reader groups related to your genre. Try to locate fans of specific authors closely related to yours or ask (when allowed in groups) about seeking reviewers.

If you know of genre-related websites such as blogs or other avenues to hit up, get at it! Everybody is a potential person to whom you can send a review copy. Blogs and websites work well with an overall marketing plan (read more in the marketing section of this book). The greatest part of ARCs is the fact that not everybody gets a copy, so it'll help motivate readers to think they're special (because they are!).

REVIEW COPIES

Even after you release a book, you can continue to give copies away to potential readers who might be interested in your books. If you are writing fiction, chances are you'll be writing in a series (if not, I encourage you to do so. It helps build a fan base and people love series) and you can give the free copies away to hopefully pull them into the rest of the series.

It's a win for you because of the review and a possible new fan. It's a win for the reader because they get a free book and get to try out a new author without any risk involved. Review copies work the same as with ARCs as far as contacting people goes. Keep peddling your book out to people and you'll be able to grow your fan base one reader at a time.

STREET TEAMS

Street Teams are a bit of an advanced topic, but I figured it'd be good to mention if you plan to do this writing gig full-time and long-term. After you learn who really reviews the books you send out, you will begin to have a list of people whom you can rely on. Getting these people in one group, you'll be able to send them all a copy when the next book is available. This is a great way to build reviews quickly upon release and cuts down on the legwork with Goodreads and Facebook in regard to contacting strangers. For a long time, I always e-mailed specific people individually, asking if they'd like a review copy. This is cumbersome. Now I have a Facebook group categorized as secret and when a new book is available, I post all the available formats into the group for my reviewers to download. I can track who has seen it and weed out anyone in the group that isn't doing their part (reading and reviewing).

Street Teams are made up of the people who will cheer for you. They'll not only review on release day, they'll share, like, comment on your new release. True supporters of your work are the ones you'll want to treat nicely and keep close for the long haul.

MAKE IT FREE

There are many reasons why you would want to make a book free permanently (looking free for a short time? Look into the Promotional section of this book). If you have a series of books and want to attract new readers who might not know who you are, this is a great way to capture their attention and pull them into your series. They might get the first book free, but they'll need to pay to read the rest (i.e. books 2-4). Also, if you have a nonfiction book but want to give the book away on Amazon in order to bring them into your larger product or website, making it free can bring more people to the site.

Amazon itself doesn't offer a way to make a book permanently free through any of their author dashboard or book options, but there is a way to do it. If you publish the book on multiple platforms (like Draft2Digital), you can make it free with the other retailers. Once you verify they have made it free, you can contact Amazon and request a price match.

Include links and locations of where the book is free so Amazon can verify the price of $0.00 before making the change on their end.

CHAPTER 15
KEYWORDS AND YOU

KEYWORDS ARE WHAT WILL ALLOW readers to find you through Amazon, search engines, social media, and everywhere else online. They are an important ingredient in the fuel you need to have success, from product pages on Amazon to your profile on LinkedIn and Twitter.

Everywhere you go online, keywords are there too.

We live in a world today that is running on overdrive and

attention spans average below five seconds. To stand out the best possible way you can, you'll need to make sure you're taking advantage of the keywords.

This chapter will give you everything you need to know and provide you with step-by-step instructions on how to do just that.

WHAT THEY ARE

Targeted words or phrases that are specifically used to drive internet traffic to a webpage, product, or service. They help categorize, organize, and steer potential consumers toward a specific direction online.

WHAT THEY ARE NOT

They are not a "set it and forget it" type of thing. You have to test and see what works for your keywords. They are also not instant win buttons in which the right keywords will make you a million dollars. They are just part of the overall puzzle that will help drive your success.

One thing to note, the big no-no with keywords is keyword

stuffing. Amazon and search engines across the web will punish you if you try stuffing a bunch of keywords into your product and website pages. It's always best to play fair and it's not worth it to try to cheat the system in any way.

HOW TO FIND THEM: AMAZON

You can find keywords a few different ways. I'll start with my favorite way, which is just heading over to Amazon.com and doing a search for books similar to yours. It's important to note: only begin to type the keyword phrase you're searching. This way you can see what Amazon's recommendation engine is providing. For this example, I'm using "Christian Romance," but I'm only typing in "Christian."

Figure 15.1 ~ Searching Amazon

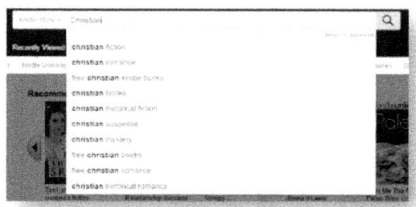

This gives a wide list of different options that are
recommended by Amazon. This helps you decide what
keyword and keyword phrases you should be focusing on.
Depending on what your keyword is, you'll be able to play
around with it. Example: With my "Christian Romance," I
would also be looking for "Inspirational Romance" and so
on. Write each keyword you like that is relatable to your
book. The closer to the top (near the box you typed in), the
more popular the keyword or keyword phrase.

Investigate each keyword by typing it into the search and
clicking the magnifying glass. I'm going to use one of the
lesser popular keywords for an example below.

Figure 15.2 – Searching Amazon

147

A list of results should populate on the screen. You will see how many books show up for that keyword in the top left corner of the search window. Over 64,000 results. As you can see from the screenshot above, there isn't much competition (people with high amounts of reviews) going on with the ones who are ranking in the first spots for the keyword "Christian fiction books." That's good, but only if there are excellent paid ranks associated with the category.

Figure 15.3 – Searching Amazon

Right after clicking in, I see it's a boxed set. According to the image used and the subtitle, I'm expecting this to be a boxed set before I scroll down to the sales rank.

Figure 15.4 – Searching Amazon

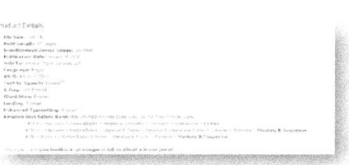

There are multiple problems once I arrive at the product details. This is supposedly a "3-in-1" boxed set, but the page count is 137. The paid rank is also horrible for being the first in the search results. This is not a winner for consumers or for us in search of a good keyword. It's time to move on.

To find a good keyword, you need to find, at least, 2-3 books that are below 10,000 paid rank (the lower the number the better) on the first couple pages of a specific keyword. You also want to make sure not every book in the results has an absurd amount of reviews in their arsenal. Reviews help sell books and if all your competition in a keyword has 200+ reviews on the first pages, chances are your keyword is likely too broad and you need to narrow down to a small audience-focused keyword or keyword phrase.

HOW TO FIND THEM: KEYWORD PLANNER

Another source of finding keywords is through Google Planner. It's a tool designed to be used in conjunction with Google AdWords, but it also works for those looking to do keyword research. You can head over to adwords.google.com/KeywordPlanner and get signed up. The process is a bit annoying the first time. You have to enter a credit card number and whatnot, but you can cancel right away. This tool isn't required to be used, so if you find the process too overwhelming or annoying, move on to the next section.

Once you've been logged into Keyword Planner, you should see something similar to the box below. Go ahead and click into the "Search for new keywords . . ." box.

Figure 15.5 – Keyword Planner

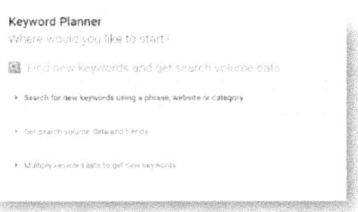

Ignore all the options inside and only type the keywords, ideas you have that are related to your product, and then press "Get Ideas." See below for my example.

Figure 15.6 – Keyword Planner Searching

You'll be taken to a dashboard like the one below. All you

need to do is click onto the tab for "Keyword ideas."

Figure 15.7 – Keyword Planner Keyword Ideas

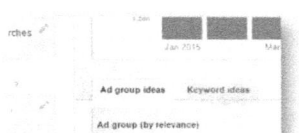

Once there, you can scroll down to your results and filter them according to search volume. You'll want to focus on traffic between 4,000 and 40,000 for a sweet spot. Note all keywords and their strength in search volume.

Return to Amazon and plug those keywords into the search up top (as shown earlier in this chapter). View the books on the first page or two and check out their paid ranks. How are they doing? Are there, at least, a few that are doing well? If not, mark that keyword off but don't toss it. You can use that keyword on your website later (for additional traffic to your books and website).

WHERE TO PLACE KEYWORDS

Keywords can be placed in your title, subtitle, summary, book cover's file name, and the name of your book file. These are all great places that will help boost your rankings within the Amazon algorithms (search engine logic). Be careful not to stuff keywords. Don't title your book "Christian Romance" and then repeat the phrase repeatedly through your description. Keep the keywords in mind and sprinkle them in where you can.

CHAPTER 16
PAGE OPTIMIZATION

MAKING SURE THAT YOUR PAGE works for you on

Amazon (and other retailers and your website) is of vital

importance. If a reader can't figure out what your book is

within a few moments of seeing your cover and landing on

your book's product page, you lose them.

Hooking and pulling in that new reader takes precision and

dedication to your presentation. It has to be perfect or you'll lose them. In this chapter, we'll be primarily focused on Amazon, but you can adapt many of these same concepts to other retailers.

Having a clean and good-looking presentation isn't where it stops; you also need visibility. Making sure you have the pieces of the puzzle all lined up will help improve your chances for success with your book. That doesn't mean you can just "set it and forget it" afterward, but you will be a step closer achieving success in self-publishing.

BOOK TITLE & SUBTITLE

The book's title and subtitle are important. If you can work a keyword into your title (easier for nonfiction), do it! If you haven't already read about keywords, go back to the "Keywords and You" chapter and learn about them. You don't want to lose out on every possible avenue in which you can increase your SEO (Search Engine Optimization). Take a look at one of my titles in the example below.

Figure 16.1 ~ Tile and Subtitle

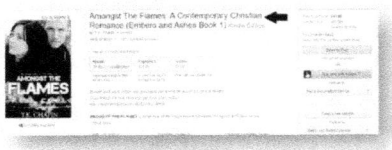

While I wasn't able to use the keyword in the actual title, I was able to include it within the subtitle. This will help increase your visibility and odds of people finding you. Be sure to optimize your title and subtitle for maximum exposure.

FORMATS & CREATING VALUE

Having multiple formats available (paperback, audiobook, and e-book) will not only help increase your credibility, it'll also give you multiple avenues to utilize keywords and funnel people to your book. It also enables the reader to consume the content however they prefer. Having the price of the paperback next to the Kindle version is also going to show them how much they could save by picking up the book digitally.

Figure 16.2 – Formats and Value

PRICING YOUR BOOK

The pricing of your e-book can make or break you, so it's
important to spend time thinking about it. If you already
have an established audience, you can play with the price
and see if you can increase it more. If it's part of a series and
it's Book One, it would be wise to make it free permanently
(see *Make it Free* section in Chapter 14 Now Give It Away) or
make it $0.99 to help lower the barrier between you as an
author and new readers. Both these strategies have their
advantages and trial and error should be done to maximize
exposure and readership.

To gain the maximum percentage of royalty from Amazon,

you must price your book between $2.99 and $9.99. Doing so will net you 70 percent of the price. At $0.99 you only get 35 percent and it's considered a "loss leader." An e-book priced at $0.99 all the time should be a book that will lead customers to purchase other books (or products) from you.

Figure 16.3 – Pricing

Look at the best sellers in your genre and categories to determine a good price point for your book. Also, note that some well-established authors and publishers might be charging a bit more than the other books. Use the smaller price points for a reference and adjust accordingly. If you price your book high (for whatever reason), the nice thing about it is you can go and decrease it later. There's no set-in-stone pricing and that's the nice thing about self-publishing. You can adjust prices for your e-book whenever you feel like doing so (promotions, price decreases, etc. . . .)

REVIEWS

Reviews are one of the most important aspects to how well your book sells. It's essential for potential readers to feel confident enough to purchase your book. Even at $0.99, they have something to lose. Building up reviews will help separate you from other books and help you stand out.

Give away as many review copies of your book (see more in Chapter 14 Now Give It Away). Don't be afraid to give your book away for nothing in these early stages of writing and publishing. You're building value for your book and yourself as an author. Give it away as much as you can until you hit a healthy number of reviews.

Figure 16.4 – Reviews

One way of setting a goal for a number of reviews would be to aim for a specific amount and adjust after you hit it. Aim for 10, 20, 30, 50, and if you want, go for 100. After 100 reviews, you should start to see a nice shift. Even 50 reviews can do that. Don't let yourself think that simply running a free promotion on your book will get you reviews. Some *might* review, but it's usually about 1 in every 1,000 free downloads in my experience. Focus on finding people to provide review copies to instead of just wishing and hoping for others to review your book.

Pro-Tip: Don't focus too much on what reviewers say. If it's positive, pat yourself on the back, but not too much. If it's negative, see if there's any useful information to improve your skills. Never respond to reviews. It's unprofessional.

COVER

We talked about the book cover earlier in this book (see Chapter 12 Book Covers), but I have to mention it again. It's important to have a stellar cover that not only tells the story but stands out in a good way. Yes, you want something similar to the best sellers out there, but you want it to be unique on your way up the charts.

CATEGORIES

When you're setting up your book in the Amazon KDP Dashboard, you'll be able to select categories. These categories will determine where you are put in the charts. Also, the keywords you use when setting up your book will also determine the categories into which you are placed. There's another step you can take if you don't find your book in the categories you wish.

Figure 16.5 – Categories

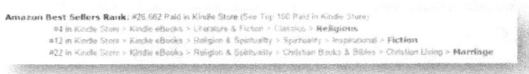

If you contact Amazon KDP support

(kdp.amazon.com/help) through the "Contact Us" option at

the bottom, you can request a category change. You'll need

to let them know which book you want to change (give

them the URL), the category you would like to change *from*

and the category you wish to change *to*.

Here's an example of the message you could send.

Figure 16.6 – E-mail KDP Support

Changing categories this way can take a little extra effort on

your part, but the payoff is worth it and I'll explain why.

You might belong in Contemporary Christian Romance, but if you can appear in Inspirational Fiction (closely related), you'll rank better and possibly be on the first page of best sellers. The reason is because of the paid ranks in the more "niche" categories. Getting into the top 20 of the best sellers is essential if you wish to maximize your profits and exposure.

Make sure you're not ranking in categories that are not related to your book. If you sell sci-fi, don't try to rank for inspirational romance. Nothing will garner negative reviews quicker than misplaced categories and readers accidently reading your book thinking it was something else.

BOOK DESCRIPTION

After a potential reader sees the cover and decides to click into your page, they'll look at your product description to see if it's a book they'll be interested in. You already hooked them by the cover, now it's time to seal the deal.

Figure 16.7 – Book Description

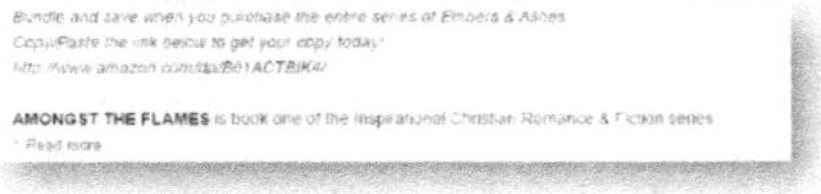

You need the description to grab the potential reader's attention immediately. They only get a glimpse of your product description when they land on the page. You should tell them immediately what your book is about. In the example above, they know immediately it's part of a series and they have the option to pick up the entire series for one low price. Change and test various starts in your description to see what hooks people into purchasing.

BOOKS IN A SERIES

Amazon's automation often has difficulties getting books of the same series all together so to help them speed this process up, I recommend you contact them once you have more than one book out in the same series. This will help bring visibility to your other titles and maximize the efficiency of your product page.

Figure 16.8 – Series

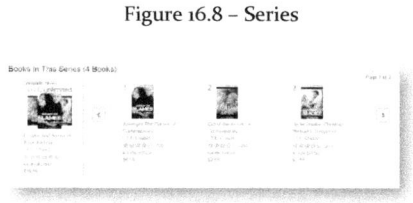

If you contact Amazon KDP support

(kdp.amazon.com/help) through the "Contact Us" option at

the bottom, you can send them a message about the series

and getting the book(s) all lumped together. Often you'll

need to do this with every book in a series to get them to

show up properly on each book's product page. Amazon's

automation process might lump them up eventually, but

you'll be in a hurry, most likely, to see them come together.

AUTHOR PAGE

Once your book has been published, it's important to head

over to authorcentral.amazon.com and claim your book

under your author profile. (Learn more on how to set up an

author profile in Chapter 13 How to Publish the Book if you

haven't already set one up.)

Figure 16.9 – Author Page

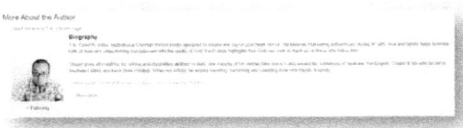

Once you claim your book, your face and bio will show up on your book's product page. This will help increase your search-ability (SEO) within Amazon and add to the optimization of your book. Everything works together to help maximize exposure for your books and you as an author.

CHAPTER 17
FREE PROMOTIONS

IF YOU DON'T PLAN TO PROMOTE, you'll sink into the

endless sea of books that are out there. There's plenty of

promoting to be done and it's not all just about spending

money. Just having a conversation with someone on the

street is promoting if done correctly. It's not a suggestion

when it comes to promoting, it's a requirement. With

millions of e-books on the market, you have to be able to

stand out and do so in a good way.

I'll start with the free avenues you can use to promote. Free is always a little easier on the pocketbook (duh), but it's often a time sink. It boils down to how much your time is worth. You can work your butt off promoting your books, and by that I mean 3-4 hours a day and barely get a couple sales, if that, *or* you could pay someone (or a company) with an audience or mailing list related to your genre and thus garner more sales (not guaranteed, but more likely than your efforts). With that being said, let's jump into free promotions.

Please note: In the back of this book is a free gift offer that contains a promotional checklist for you. It contains both free and paid promotion tactics that will help maximize the impact of your promotion.

GOODREADS

Goodreads.com is a community of over forty million members with over 1.3 billion books that have been added. I'd suggest finding groups related to your genre (e.g. Christian romance, fantasy, etc. . . .) and then also find groups with discounted or Kindle Unlimited Reads (if your book is Amazon exclusive).

Another way you can promote through Goodreads is to host a giveaway in which you offer one (or more) lucky winner(s) a paperback copy of your book. This is a good way to attract new readers and get people thinking about your book.

FACEBOOK

Find niche groups on Facebook. You can search for them by typing in Kindle books, free books, e-books, and so on. Join the groups that allow self-promoting (they often post rules about it). This won't yield a whole lot of results since most of the groups consist of only other authors, but the niche groups can really grab traction if you find the right groups. There are a few great Christian groups with low numbers in them, but they have great user activity and engagement. It's all about finding your people (readers). This tactic can often feel time-consuming without much result. If you want to know how well the groups are doing, or any self-promoting you are doing, I recommend using a website like www.bitly.com that will track clicks to Amazon so you can gauge the usefulness. It'll also shorten your links, which is nice to save room in your messages that you send out to the masses.

TWITTER

Don't just use Twitter to spam your book promotion. Instead, post frequently with automated software such as www.hootsuite.com and retweet with www.roundteam.co. Neither requires money and both keep you active on Twitter without always being at the keyboard, tweeting. When you promote your book, use keywords (see Chapter 15 Keywords and You for more info) and try to capture the possible readers' attention. You can use others' tweets as inspiration to see what you should do. I'd keep a good ratio between retweets of others, useful information or articles and then promotion tweets. Only sprinkle in your self-promoting or you'll lose followers.

Example of promo tweet: BOOK BARGAIN ALERT! Only $0.99 for a limited time – Amongst the Flames. http://amzn.to/21B4sEg #99cents #romance #mustread

Here's a list of hashtags related to writing. Your book's genre will make this list larger, but here are some generic ones and a few genre-specific ones to get you started.

#Books

#140Poem

#99c

#99cents

#Amazon

#AuthorRT

#BookBuzzr

#BookGiveaway

#BookMarketing

#BookPromo

#BookWorm

#Comedy

#Crime

#DarkFantasy

#Dystopian

#eBook

#ePubChat

#eReaders

#FaithLitChat

#FollowFriday

#FreebieFriday

#FreeReads

#GreatReads

#HistFic

#Historical

#IndieThursday

#iPad

#KidLitChat

#Kindle

#KindleBargain

#Kobo

#KPD (Kindle Publishing Direct)

#Literature

#LitFic

#MemoirChat

#MGLit (middle grades literature)

#MustRead

#Mystery

#NonFiction

#Nook

#Novel

#Novelines

#Paperbacks

#Paranormal

#Poetry

#PoetryMonth (Each April in the USA)

#Pubit

#Romantic

#RomanticSuspense

#sale

#ScienceFiction

#SciFiChat

#ShortStory

#SmashWords

#Sony

#SteamPunk

#Storytelling

#Suspense

#TrueStories

#UrbanFantasy

#Webfic

#WhatToRead

#WomensFiction

#YA

#YALit

You'll also want to tweet to book promoters. Some accounts won't reply, but many will promote if your book is a good fit for them. You'll have to search Twitter for accounts related to your genre or niche or do broad searches on keywords such as "free book promo" and find accounts to tweet. Track and record data on the ones that retweet you and you'll be able to see who retweets and who doesn't. Here's a small list to get you started on some I've used in the past.

@CrazyKindle

@CheapKindleBks

@cheapbooksdaily

@amzn_deal

@bestdealskindle

@ShopKindleDeals

@KindleDailyDeal

@Dailycheapreads

@kindledeals

@KindleDeals

@eReadingCheap

@AllKindleDeals

@CheapKindleBook

@99centfinds

@cheapkindle1

@KindleCheap

REDDIT

Reddit.com is a website with large communities built
around niche topics. You can find some of the groups to be
useful, but be sure to follow each community's rules. To
find Reddit boards, head over to Google.com and search
"title" Reddit.

Once you figure where you'll post on Reddit, you'll want to
come up with a catchy title. Be sure to use keywords (see

the keywords chapter for more info).You can use others'

posts as inspiration to see what you should do.

Example: [Kindle] Inspirational Christian Fiction – After the

Fire (Only $0.99)

BLOGS

Probably one of the most efficient ways to promote your

book without it costing you anything is to contact blogs

related to the niche your book belongs in. If you can find

blogs with a decent amount of traffic going to it and they're

willing to read/review your book, you're striking gold.

Tapping into their traffic is an excellent way to pull people

to your books. These bloggers have built relationships with

their readers and when they recommend a book, they're

telling others to buy your book. Be careful not to waste your

time with blogs that have zero to three people worth of

traffic, though. They'll often not be worth the effort that's involved with coming up with original content for their blog (oftentimes the blog will want you to provide content outside of the book link).

If you do manage to find a blog with great traffic that's also open to books and guest posts, be kind and friendly in your e-mail to them. You'll want to state exactly what the purpose of your appearance on the blog is, what kind of value you could offer (tip/trick/free promo day). DO NOT SEND YOUR BOOK until it's requested. This is a huge assumption on your part and you shouldn't just be tossing your content out there like that when you haven't spoken to them. Some bloggers will ignore you entirely.

With an adequate amount of effort on your part, guest posting and reviews on blogs within your niche can be a huge advantage to your book and your name as an author.

OTHER PLACES

Here are some other places you can promote your book(s) without it costing you a dime. You can also find the full list at benjaminchapin.com/writing-tools/.

- http://www.amazon.com/forum/meet%20our%20auth ors/ref=cm_cd_t_mdb_f?_encoding=UTF8&cdForum= Fx2UYC1FC06SU8S&tag=vglnkc7974-20

- http://awesomegang.com/submit-your-book/

- http://www.bestebooksfree.com/Authors-eBook-Promotion.shtml

- http://bookgoodies.com/bargain-books/

- http://bookpinning.com/?sws=home/submit-book

- https://docs.google.com/forms/d/1DlL2gaFaDtcTbjZST E-zsGD4HOvHRccShMyycCgqfGs/viewform

- http://www.ebooklister.net/submit.php

- http://ereaderutopia.com/

- http://www.feedyourreader.com/submit-your-book-2/

- http://www.kuforum.co.uk/guide#authors

- http://pinyourbook.com/

- http://readingdeals.com/submit-ebook

CHAPTER 18
PAID PROMOTIONS

PAID PROMOTION WILL EXPOSE YOU to readers like no other way will. Some of the promotion companies, such as BookBub, can change people's lives when they (the promotion company) decide to promote a book. It can be hard to invest the money when you first approach the idea, but after you see successful promotions, you'll wonder why you didn't do it sooner.

There was a long stint in my career where I wasn't able to do any paid promotions and my writing career suffered greatly because of it. Once you start investing in your books, you start investing in yourself. You'll be able to gain new readers and reach your audience on levels you only dreamed of previously.

Please note: In the back of this book is a free gift offer that contains a promotional checklist for you. It contains both free and paid promotion tactics that will help maximize the impact of your promotion.

PROMOTIONAL SITES

I'll show you exactly what websites that offer promotions you can use for your paid promotions. While these are not guaranteed to make your money back, it's wise to try them out.

<u>My Favorites:</u>

BookBub (The Ultimate) – (www.bookbub.com/partners)

Ereader News Today (www.ereadernewstoday.com)

Faithful Reads (Christian) –

(www.faithfulreads.com/authors/)

Bknights at Fiverr (www.fiverr.com/bknights)

Fussy Librarian (http://www.thefussylibrarian.com/for-authors/)

Buck Books (Nonfiction) (www.buckbooks.net/buck-books-promotions/)

There are plenty more websites, but this should get you started. For a more in-depth list, please visit benjaminchapin.com/writing-tools/. Each time you run a paid promotion it'll be important to track the data and see what kind of results you generate during the run. Keeping track of this data will be important as you will be able to determine what was worth your money and what wasn't. Some websites, like Buck Books, do well with nonfiction but not so good with fiction. Testing and keeping notes will save you time and money in the long run.

BookBub

The promotional site BookBub requires its own special note. It's of vital importance to your success as an author. There are plenty of authors who have found success without it, but if you're able to get a book accepted into BookBub, it'll be worth every dime. It's the one website that can change your life by a promotional run. I went from struggling daily with sales and almost being to a point where I was looking at getting a job to a record-breaking month by a single BookBub run. Now, because of BookBub, I haven't had to think about getting a day job at all.

While their promotions are expensive, they are worth every penny and there is absolutely no way you can be accepted into BookBub and not make a return on investment (though it's not guaranteed). Even at $200+ for a single e-mail blast (learn more about pricing at www.bookbub.com/partners/pricing) you make money. I made all my record-breaking sales months on a free book being promoted!

I would recommend subscribing to BookBub for your genre and studying everything you can about the books that are being listed in the daily e-mails. See how many reviews they have, see how they wrote their blurb—watch, read, and mimic success in your own way.

Getting into BookBub is extremely difficult. Many of the books they feature in their e-mail blasts are New York Times Bestsellers, but they promote both traditionally published and self-published, so you do have a chance. I could write an entire book on this website alone, but I won't. Here's my best guess on getting accepted into BookBub (I've been in several times).

1. Subscribe and study your genre that's being featured daily.

2. You should already have a perfect copy of your manuscript, but if you see reviews mentioning problems, get them fixed and fire the editor in question. You need perfection when approaching BookBub.

3. Study the Requirements (www.bookbub.com/partners/requirements)

4. Fine-tune your book description and use the books being featured from BookBub in the e-mail as a source of inspiration to make tweaks.

5. Earn reviews, lots of them. Try to get some of the Amazon Top Reviewers (www.amazon.com/review/top-reviewers) to read and review your book.

6. Get more reviews! Seriously. Go find bloggers and build your reviews up to the roof. You need critical

reviews and reviews from well-known sources to help increase your chances.

7. Submit and pray for a miracle.

Some authors spend years trying to get into BookBub and others can find themselves in a featured e-mail within months of trying. It's all up to the editors at BookBub to decide who gets in and who doesn't. I recommend aiming for a free feature with them; it's easier to get picked if you go that route. If you write in a series (fiction) I would wait until you have a couple books out and hammer home that first one on trying to get in. A first in a series on BookBub is gold.

FACEBOOK PROMOTIONS

If you have some cash for marketing and want to try something different outside of promotional sites, you can set up an ad through Facebook.

The first thing you'll want to do if you plan on using the

Facebook ad to send people to a product page for a book on

Amazon is go get signed up for Amazon Associates at

affiliate-program.amazon.com (using your Amazon

account). Having an account will allow you to track clicks to

Amazon and purchases.

Please note: This process takes a while and you are

required to enter a website URL (your author website

URL) for sign-up.

Figure 18.1 – Create Ads

This will help you gauge the success of your Facebook ad.

Without signing up for this account, you'll have no way of

knowing what clicks were purchases. Once signed up, find

your book through the dashboard, and locate the affiliate

URL.

If you don't have a website or wish not to sign up, that's okay. Facebook will provide you with "clicks" data and other demographics. The downside of the data they provide you is that it doesn't show anything about whether the person who clicked purchased the book or not (that's why the affiliate link is nice).

<u>Facebook Ad – The How To:</u>

1.   Go to Create Ads.

Figure 18.2 – Create Ads

2.   Select "Send People to Your Website" (if promoting book).

3. Enter the URL for your book (or use your affiliate link) and name your campaign. Ignore the pixel code message, as you won't be using it.

Figure 18.3 – Campaign Name

4. Click through options and you'll come to setting up an audience: this is called your ad set. These options will be where you specifically target people to whom the ad will be shown. It's important you know your audience. Even with a healthy understanding of your reader, you'll spend some time testing different ad sets until you find ones

that produce great results. Track all your test

audiences and adjust accordingly.

Figure 18.4 – Audience Ad Set

In the above example (visit

benjaminchapin.com/writing-tools/ for bigger images)

you can see I narrowed my audience clear down to

83,000 total people. This is probably a bit too narrow. It

really depends on how far you want your reach to be.

The larger the audience, the more possibilities you have

for clicks, but the less likely a conversion will happen.

It's important to spend a good deal of time closely

monitoring and adjusting ads to maximize their

efficiency.

5. Scroll down to your budget. This is important because you do not want to accidently set the standards at $20/day or $350-lifetime budget. In the beginning, you'll want to make tiny budgets so you can test out ads before ramping them up full steam.

Figure 18.5 – Budget Ad Set

I recommend starting around $5. You'll want to make several different ads, and even at $5 each, your cost will grow rapidly. Be careful and have fun. Once you're finished, name the ad set at the bottom for future uses.

6. Next, you'll be setting up your image.

Recommended Image Specs

- Recommended image size: 1200 x 628 pixels

- Image ratio: 1.91:1

- Your image may not include more than 20-percent
  text.

- Square Crop (1:1) is recommended for the Instagram
  placement.

Figure 18.6 – Images

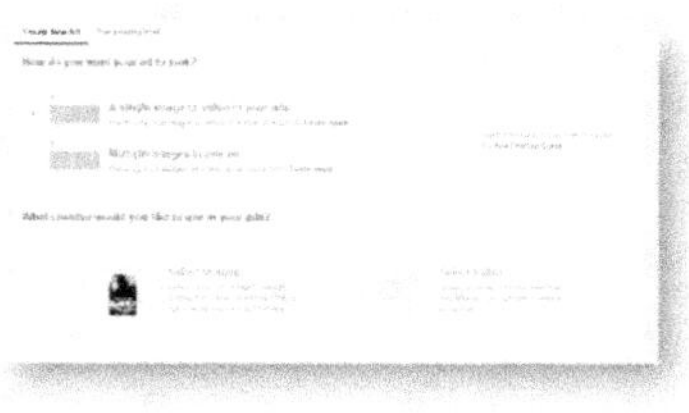

In the above screenshot (visit

benjaminchapin.com/writing-tools/ for a bigger image

or if you're listening on audiobook), you can see you

have the option to add an image, multiple images, or

video. Usually, one image is good, but it's up to you. If

you have multiple images to test or want to experiment, I recommend adding them here. When you click into "Single Image," a menu will appear and you can add stock photos (free) or add your own (that are stored on your computer).

7. Scroll down. Now you'll need to set up the ad.

Figure 18.7 – Ad Set-up

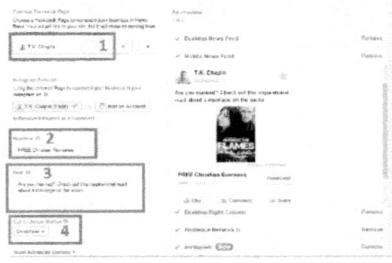

1. Select the Author Page you set up through Chapter 20 Let's Get Social.

2. Create a catchy headline that will grab readers' attention.

3. Text here needs to motivate whoever sees it to stop. One of the easiest ways to do this is asking a

question they'll say "yes" to (example: are you married?). Then, explain exactly what you're offering. For more on ad copy, I'd suggest checking out this amazing read at www.clairepells.com/facebook-ad-copy/.

4. Choose a Call to Action Button text for your ad. Then you're done. Just place your order and enter payment information. Facebook is a secure website and will protect your credit or debit card information. If you feel worried, you can also use PayPal, which is also secure.

Please note: you need to be careful when you are making ads on Facebook. Keep an eye on your billing information and threshold. You don't want to end up spending money you don't have and get hit with a big, unexpected payment. Facebook will automatically charge your account if you don't make the payment

upon the agreed threshold or cycle.

OTHER PROMOTIONS

If you are on the hunt for other promotions not listed here,

you can visit www.kboards.com and go to the Writer's Café

in the Authors section. They have loads of researched

promotions and even genre-specific tactics that work.

Each genre works differently. For example, I write in

Christian Fiction & Romance and have struggled to find

good sources of advertising. Some sites that work for horror

and fantasy might not necessarily work so well for Christian.

It's all a trial-and-error game when it comes to paid and free

promotions. Do the homework and spend your money

wisely to get the best impact for your dollar. As long as

you're not setting and forgetting books, you should be able

to find the traction you need.

CHAPTER 19
AMAZON PROMOTIONS INFORMATION

AMAZON OFFERS TOOLS FOR AUTHORS that every new author should be utilizing as they set foot into the self-publishing industry. I know (because I was there) how appealing the idea of being at every possible retailer sounds, but take my word on it—it's not that great. You have two options when you go to publish. You can publish on Amazon exclusively and get all the benefits (I'll cover that in this chapter), or you can publish across multiple retailers and most likely make less money for a long time. The idea of being on Google Play, iBooks, Barnes & Noble, and beyond might sound great but in all my experience, it's not. Still to this day, the majority of my titles are exclusive to Amazon and page reads attribute to, at least, 20-30 percent of my income.

In this chapter, I'll show you what Amazon offers and you can do as you wish. I'll also cover the reporting system that is built into Amazon and how that works.

If you have questions about Kindle Countdown, Free Promo Days, and Kindle Unlimited; this is the chapter for you. I'll cover all the goodness and then a little bit more.

Please note: Only Amazon exclusive titles (Kindle Direct Publishing Select) are eligible for all the promotional tools discussed in this chapter. It's on a per-book basis, not per account. Every ninety days the author has an opportunity to enroll or un-enroll in the KDP.

FREE DAYS

If you choose to use the five free days Amazon provides, you'll be ineligible for the Kindle Countdown Deals (discussed later in this chapter) during your KDP cycle. It's best to line up paid promotions and then have an attack plan for the free ways to promote on the day your book is free. I have found one or two days to be the best when using free promo days. Other people have had luck with running a full five-day stint at once. Test and see what works for you. Each free book given away will be tracked on your Amazon dashboard in the reports section. Use these reports to track success and fails of your promotional tactics.

Please note: If you use these free days, make sure you're not overusing them or you'll collect so-

called fans that only get your books when they're free.

KINDLE COUNTDOWN

Kindle Countdowns are a way to mark your book down for a discounted price without missing out on the royalty percentage that you would normally receive. Say for example if you do a Kindle Countdown for your book to be $0.99, normally you'd only receive 30 percent of the price (if discounted manually), but with Kindle Countdown, you'll be netting the same 70 percent (assuming your book is normally priced between $2.99-$9.99). It's a neat way to lower prices without dropping your royalties to the floor. You can run Kindle Countdowns every ninety days, just like free days, but you have seven days' worth of Kindle Countdown time instead of five like the free days.

You'll be able to track sales specific to your promotion through the promotion area of the reports tab on your

Amazon dashboard.

KINDLE UNLIMITED & PRIME

Prime is a membership that Amazon customers can sign up for to receive discounted items, free shipping, and other goodies, which include a free book loan each month. That book will be read and reported through the Amazon dashboard just like Kindle Unlimited.

Kindle Unlimited is, basically, a subscription service (such as Netflix) for books at Amazon. It's available in most parts of the world and growing. It's a subscription-based service that allows readers to check your book out (they're allowed up to 10 books out at a time). When you sign up for KDP Select (to be exclusive with Amazon), you are automatically enrolled into this program and people are allowed to borrow your book.

Each month you'll earn what is called page reads and will be paid according to that number. Amazon pays out on a per-page basis and they split a giant pot divided among all the pages read. Each month is similar to a lottery as you wait to find out how much worth a page is going to be. It's been hovering around $0.0040-$0.0050 for a while now (as of March 2016). While Amazon doesn't provide the payout information on the pages per their website, they do make announcements in the KDP forums letting people know what the monthly global fund was for the previous month. You can see an example here (kdp.amazon.com/community/ann.jspa?annID=973). The Kindle Unlimited program has gone through several changes and I'm sure it's going to keep changing until the dust settles one day in the future. You'll be able to track page reads through the reports dashboard (learn more in Chapter 13 How to Publish the Book).

CHAPTER 20
LET'S GET SOCIAL

BUILDING YOUR PLATFORM ON SOCIAL media is going

to be an important step in the process as you build your

author platform. Having social media accounts is important.

Some social media sites might not be as important as others

for your genre or goals, but there are some basic ones that

should be used by every author.

In this chapter, we'll cover the basics of Facebook and

Twitter. Other sites like LinkedIn and Google+ are good to be on, but I've never felt it as important as the two mentioned above. I'll also be going over some basic tactics you can use while using social media platforms that were lightly covered in Chapter 17 Free Promotions.

FACEBOOK: SETUP

As an author, you'll want to be on Facebook first and foremost. This will give your readers a way to connect with you outside of the books. You can use this author page not only to connect but to promote and reveal more about the person behind the pen (metaphorical pen of course unless you're a quill-and-paper kind of author).

1. Go to www.facebook.com/pages/create

2. Click "Artist, Band or Public Figure."

Figure 20.1 – Fan Page Set-up

3. Select Author from the drop-down and click get

   started.

Figure 20.2 – Setup Cont.

4. On the next screen, you'll be prompted to fill out the

   information.

Figure 20.3 – Setup Cont.

Fill this out accurately and use keywords. With only a few sentences available, you won't be able to put as much as in your author profile at Author Central, but you should have enough room to add details. Also, enter your domain URL for your author website and pick a URL ending for your author page. Usually just setting it as "authorname" should work unless it's taken; if it is, use another style, "author[AuthorName]."

Example: facebook.com/authortkchapin

5. Go through the rest of the options with the standard defaults. Once you are finished, Facebook will offer you a tour around your page to show you the ropes.

Once your page is all set up and looking nice (customized and purdy), go ahead and start self-promoting your new page. Push aside that awkward feeling of self-promotion and share it to your timeline. Then go and share it with the world by inviting friends. Some will like it and some will not. It's not a big deal. You're working on your dream; don't worry about the unsupportive people.

Figure 20.4 – Invite Friends

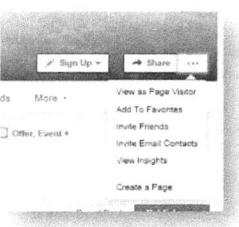

FACEBOOK: LONG TERM

After you get everything set up, make a note of your
Facebook fan page URL. This will be on all your e-mails, on
your website, and in the back of every book you publish.
Keep things connected—always. You want people to be able
to reach you however they wish.

The long-term goal of your Facebook page is going to be
connecting with readers and revealing who you are. You can
also toss in some promotion here and there to let those
people who may not be signed up on the mailing list know
about you and your book(s) (more on mailing list in
Chapter 22 E-mail Marketing).

TWITTER: SETUP

Twitter setup is relatively easy. If you already have a Twitter
account and you're not using a pseudonym, you can just use
that. Otherwise, you'll need to go through the new account
setup using the name you desire. You can sign up by visiting
www.twitter.com/signup.

TWITTER: LONG TERM

Twitter is a way you can connect with fans who want to follow you, share information or articles, and be another avenue for your promotions. It's going to act in a lot of the same ways as Facebook. You'll want to have a link to your Twitter on your website, in your e-mails, and in the back of your books as well.

SOCIAL MEDIA TOOLS: HOOTSUITE

Hootsuite.com is a website that helps you deliver content via scheduled tweets and posts. You can sign up for a free account that is limited, but still useful.

1. Sign up at www.hootsuite.com

2. Click into dashboard.

3. Click into the Compose Message area at the top.

Figure 20.5 – Hootsuite

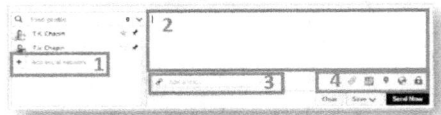

1. Click "Add social network" to link up an account.

2. Compose your message.

3. Add a link if applicable.

4. You can add a picture, schedule, location, etc. . . .

5. Once you're happy with your message, hit Send Now,
    or if it's scheduled, it'll say Schedule.

Please note: Hootsuite has a variety of options, but most of them (like bulk scheduling and analytics) are for paid accounts.

I don't recommend using Hootsuite to just schedule promotional content. Instead, post related topics and interests that would be applicable to your core audience (niche). Don't overload them with articles and whatnot, either. If you do, they'll ignore or unfollow you. Play it cool and experiment. If you're curious about the paid features, you can always sign up for a month and try it out. Sometimes they have a free trial, otherwise it's $10/month for the basic access to the pro tools.

SOCIAL MEDIA TOOLS: ROUNDTEAM

RoundTeam.co is another tool, but it's exclusively for Twitter (Hootsuite works for multiple platforms). It's nice because it allows you to retweet tweets to help you appear more active when you really aren't. This shouldn't be abused, but it comes in handy when it comes to promotion. If you've been retweeting other like-minded authors and you push out a promotional tweet, they'll likely retweet you to return the favor.

This is a free application, but they do offer pricing options for more unlocked features and abilities.

1. Go to www.roundteam.co

2. Click the sign in with Twitter and authorize the app.

3. In a separate window, bring up www.twitter.com

4. On Twitter, find the accounts you'd like to retweet (usually genre specific to your book(s) or industry, other authors, etc. . . .).

5. Click on the gear icon and then on "Add or remove from lists."

Figure 20.6 – Roundteam.co and Twitter Setup

6. Create List (or select list if you already have one).

7. Do this for as many people as you wish (all on one list).

8. Go back to the window with the Round Team Dashboard up and click the "+" symbol near the bottom.

Figure 20.7 – Roundteam.co and Twitter Setup Cont.

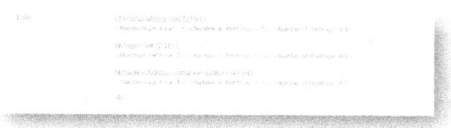

9. In the list name enter: [TwitterID]/[NameOfList]
   (Replace TwitterID with just your username. For
   example, mine is: tkchapin and for the list name,
   whatever you created in the earlier steps). Refer to the
   image above for help.

10. Customize the rest as you see fit and save. Now Round
    Team will retweet on your behalf.

CONCLUSION

No matter what services you use, don't give up trying
different tactics and analyzing data when you can.
Sometimes a small tweak can be a game changer. Be aware
of your social presence and attack the fires you see and test

always. Don't become stale and automated in everything you do. People can tell you are when you post a tweet and Facebook update at 2 a.m. about loving summertime (really happened to me once thanks to my virtual assistant).

CHAPTER 21
AUTHOR WEBSITES

PEOPLE ARE GOING TO LOOK for you online as an

author, and it's important to have a website up and running,

and not a free one. I've seen many authors with free

websites that are hosted through places like Weebly and

WordPress, but I don't advise you do that. It's relatively

inexpensive to get a website domain address and web

hosting up and running. Don't worry if you don't

understand that lingo right now; by the end of this chapter you'll get it.

BUYING A DOMAIN & HOSTING

First, I will explain what a domain is. If you've been reading this book, you've seen me reference my website (www.benjaminchapin.com). That's a domain or domain URL. The domain is the website address, just like your house has an address. Hosting is the place it's being held, just like the land your house is on.

If you're new to the world of buying domains and running websites, you're lucky. You can snag a domain URL over at GoDaddy.com for $1-$3 by simply looking for a GoDaddy coupon on Google. I'll walk you through getting started with GoDaddy.com.

1. Head over to www.godaddy.com (after you get your cheap domain code from Google).

2. Click "Sign In" at the top and then click "Create My Account."

Figure 21.1 – GoDaddy Sign Up

3. Fill in the information required.

4. Once logged in, go to www.godaddy.com/domains

5. Search for the domain you wish to own and click "Select" (try your author name you're using first, preferably). If it's not available, try to add author or something along those names until you can secure one that is either a .com or .net extension. There's a large list of extensions offered, but often people associate

other extensions (.me, .info, etc. . .) with being less

credible. Ultimately it's up to you.

Figure 21.2 – GoDaddy Domain pick

6. GoDaddy offers you a variety of options. I'd

   recommend skipping it all and proceeding directly to

   the checkout.

7. Once in the checkout, click the "Hosting" tab up top

   and select Web Hosting.

Figure 21.3 – GoDaddy Pick Web Hosting

8. Select WordPress Hosting up at the top. Then scroll down to the Basic Option. The prices change randomly, so don't use this picture as a baseline. Usually, they give you a nice discount for the first month.

Figure 21.4 – GoDaddy Hosting Select

9. GoDaddy will offer you a discount if you lock in the commitment for a year. This is up to you.

10. Once back in the shopping cart, adjust the terms you'd like to have (GoDaddy often defaults to long term periods). Enter your coupon code in the area to the right.

Figure 21.5 – GoDaddy Check out: Terms & Coupon Code

11. Click Proceed to Checkout and finish the order. Congratulations! You've purchased your domain and hosting. Now you should be able to proceed into GoDaddy and manage your website. Each month your hosting will

need to be renewed using your payment on file unless you paid a long-term fee. GoDaddy.com usually automatically renews your hosting unless you turn this auto-renewal off. Your domain will be valid for a year unless you selected longer.

WEBSITE: INSTALLING WORDPRESS

Now that you've purchased the domain and hosting, make sure you're logged into your GoDaddy account. Then head into the Web Hosting part of your account. You need to install a CMS (Content Management System). Think of this as the house that will be going on your patch of property (hosting). We'll use WordPress because it's fast, easy, and user-friendly.

1. Select the Manage option next to the hosting account you want to manage (you should only have one unless you bought more stuff in the past).

2. In the Popular Apps section, click "WordPress."

3. Click "Install Now."

4. Complete the on-screen fields and click "OK."

     a. Domain – You should select the domain you just created.

     b. Directory – The only thing that this should have is a "/" entered.

     c. Enter a username, a password (and its confirmation), and an e-mail address. (Please write this down somewhere safe).

WordPress will be installed to your hosting account and it can take up to 24 hours to fully install. Once it's completed, you'll be e-mailed.

WEBSITE: LOGGING INTO WORDPRESS FOR THE FIRST TIME

Now you are ready to go! Your website is bought (address),

your hosting has been set up (property), and even

WordPress has been installed (house). If this is your first

time ever doing this, congratulations! Now it's time to work

on making that site. I'm going to walk you through logging

in the first time.

1. Go to yourwebsite.com/wp-admin/ (replace

"yourwebsite.com" with your actual domain) and type

in your credentials.

Figure 21.6 – WordPress Login

2. Congratulations! You are now logged into your site!

Creating your website is all personal preference as far as the look and design so I recommend you watch some different videos if you're new to WordPress and would like to learn more about the process. You can always look up tutorials, videos, and so on, yourself, beyond this book. I have provided a link below to get you started.

WordPress Video Tutorials: https://youtu.be/8OBfr46YocQ

CHAPTER 22
E-MAIL MARKETING

HAVING A PROFESSIONAL-LOOKING WEBSITE isn't just

so you have somewhere pretty for people to look at your

books and face: it's an important ingredient in having a

successful author career. It goes hand-in-hand with your e-

mail marketing plan. You don't just want someone to read a

book of yours and forget about you, you want them to sign

up for your mailing list so you can let them know about

every release that comes out. That's where e-mail marketing and an e-mail list comes in handy.

If you watch some of the people who have been around for a long time, they can release a book and break 1,000 in the paid store (rank based on sales) by simply marketing to their list. That should be the goal of any self-published author looking to turn their writing into a life-long endeavor. Building fans and an e-mail list is where the money and long-term success is.

I recommend asking only for an e-mail address when people sign up for your mailing list. Asking for more information (name, address, etc. . . .) will only hamper your results and you'll get fewer subscribers because of it. Let's talk about the different options you have as an author. I'll go over the two biggest ones.

MAILCHIMP

MailChimp is a free e-mail service provider (if you go

beyond 2,000 subscribers, you'll need to upgrade and pay).

They can help send bulk e-mails to customers. Their

application is based on the three main tasks of e-mail

marketing: managing subscriber lists, building e-mail

campaigns, and reviewing campaign reports. I recommend

this if you would like to have something free, but please be

aware they don't have an autoresponder (automated

messages that go out to new subscribers) like AWeber does

(more on AWeber in the next section). Let's get started on

how to set up an account with MailChimp.

1. Go to www.mailchimp.com

2. Click "Sign Up" in the top right corner.

3. Enter your information.

Figure 22.1 – MailChimp Sign Up

How to Create a List and embed on your WordPress Site

1. Log into MailChimp.com dashboard and click "Lists" at the top of the screen.

Figure 22.2 – MailChimp Lists

2. Click "Create List" and fill out the details.

3. Once back in your Lists, click the arrow to the right of the list and select "Signup forms."

Figure 22.3 – MailChimp List Options

4. Select "Embedded Forms."

Figure 22.4 – MailChimp Embedded Form

5. Select the Super Slim option and scroll to bottom.

   Right click and copy the text from that box.

Figure 22.5 – MailChimp Right click and Copy

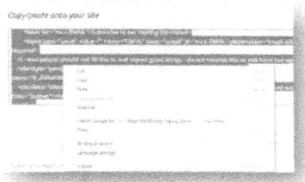

6. Open a new browser and go to your website (if you don't have a website, go back to Chapter 21 Author Websites and set one up).

7. Once logged into your admin panel (through authorwebsite.com/wp-admin/), go to the page you wish to embed the code with (or make a new one named sign-up).

8. Once on the page you wish to insert the code, click "Text" (highlighted in picture below) and then right click and paste into the body.

Figure 22.6 – MailChimp Right click and Paste

9. Before publishing, click Preview Changes on the WordPress page and see how it looks. If everything looks fine, publish.

Figure 22.7 – MailChimp Mail Sign-up Embed

Did you make it through without any issues? Congratulations! You now have a way for your fans to subscribe to your mailing list! Make sure you add this page to your website's main menu and a link to the sign-up in the back of every book. This is one of the most crucial things you can do for your author platform and it's essential to have long-term success.

When you need to notify your e-mail list, just log back into MailChimp and go to "Campaigns" at the top. You'll be able to send the same message to each subscriber.

AWEBER

AWeber is like MailChimp, but you get more out of it and it costs money. The cost is worth it for the autoresponder feature built into AWeber. For instance, when someone signs up for your mailing list, you can have follow-up messages that go out to them at set intervals of time. This works great if you have lots of content and information you want to provide to your readers, but don't necessarily want to bombard them with it all at once. I have a free devotional that I have set up that will send an e-mail every day, as long as it's not on Sunday, for an entire month after they sign up. The options and flexibility with AWeber are awesome. You can get a free month to try them out, and you start with the basic package, which is $19 a month for up to 500 subscribers, then it bumps up to $29 a month for 500-2500 and keeps going up from there. I'll walk you through how to get started.

1. Go to www.aweber.com

2. Click the green "Free Trial" button and sign up.

3. Log into AWeber dashboard and click "Manage Lists."

Figure 22.8 – AWeber Manage Lists

4. Click "Create A List."

5. Plug in your author details.

6. Name the list.

7. Customize the confirmation message with whatever you like or accept the default.

8. Approve it.

9. You should be back in the dashboard and should see your list name up at the top.

Figure 22.9 – AWeber Dashboard Top

10. Click "Signup Forms" (right under the Current List display).

11. Customize your signup form how you wish for it to look on your website. Click "Next" once completed.

Figure 22.10 – AWeber Signup Form Customize

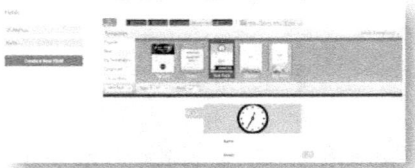

12. Pick a name for the form and customize the Thank You page (if you made one on your website, or want to showcase your books on the thank you page, I suggest setting a thank you page up on your site).

13. Time to publish this puppy! Select the "I will install My Form" option and then right click and copy the Javascript Snippet.

Figure 22.11 – AWeber Snippet Right Click - Copy

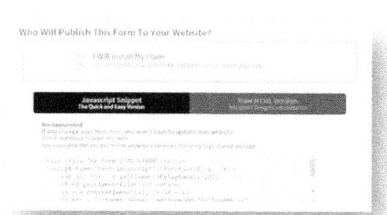

14. Open a new browser and go to your website (if you don't have a website, go back to Chapter 21 Author Websites and set one up).

15. Once logged into your admin panel (through authorwebsite.com/wp-admin/), go to the page you wish to embed the code with (or make a new one named sign-up).

16. Once on the page you wish to insert the code, click "Text" (highlighted in picture below) and then right click and paste into the body.

Figure 22.12 – AWeber Right click and Paste

17. Before publishing, click "Preview Changes" on the WordPress page and see how it looks. If everything looks fine, publish.

Did you make it through without any issues?

Congratulations! You now have a way for your fans to subscribe to your mailing list! Make sure you add this page to your website's main menu and a link to the sign-up in the back of every book. This is one of the most crucial things you can do for your author platform and is essential to have long-term success!

AWeber offers campaigns, which will send follow-up e-mails to subscribers. You can learn how to use campaigns and other features of AWeber by visiting help.aweber.com.

E-MAIL MARKETING: WHAT AND WHEN

The quickest way to lose subscribers is to start spamming them with stuff they can buy. Instead of e-mailing your list every time you think about it, have a strategy in place to maximize efficiency and keep those subscribers on your list. When you do send an e-mail, make sure it's full of useful information, freebies (if you can), or extreme discounts on books or related products.

Limit your e-mailing to 1-2 times a month. If you don't have a book available, give them a sneak peek of the book you're working on. The best thing you can do is keep enough contact that they don't forget who you are, but not so much contact that they skip over your e-mail when they see your name pop up in their inbox.

If you found some neat information related to your genre or niche, write a blog post and include it in your e-mail and then toss in the work-in-progress. Don't overthink the e-mail marketing strategy; simple is better.

When you have a new release, another thing you can do is hit up your mailing list and let them know about the preorder (if you set one up) and then offer early-bird review copies for those who preorder (request the receipt be e-mailed if you wish to verify). This will not only excite the subscribers, it'll increase the perception of value by being on the list. Always make your subscribers happy to have subscribed.

E-MAIL MARKETING: COLLECTING E-MAILS

Make sure the verbiage you use in the back of your book pulls the reader in. They have to see a value in giving up their e-mail address to sign up. It's your job to provide that value.

Example:

Sign up for the Mailing List and

be notified of new releases, promotions, and more!

Sign Up Now

Another option you might want is take the offer to the next level. If you use AWeber, you can set up an autoresponder that will automatically send out a welcome e-mail customized to that list and you can include files (such as a PDF). You can give the new subscriber tips, tricks, or a freebie of some sort. Right now, I'm currently offering a starter library for T.K. Chapin and it gives subscribers three free books to get them started. Two of the books are the first of two different series and then the other is a novella (a short novel). While you will attract freebie hunters, you will also find some gems mixed in that will go on to buy all your other books. It's a great way to build your mailing list. If you don't want to give books away, make a free report (if you are in nonfiction) or give a short story away.

Make links to your sign-up forms everywhere you are set up online (Facebook, Twitter, etc. . . . .). I'll show you how to setup a call to action (sign-up) on Facebook.

Call to Action on Facebook

1.) Go to Facebook and log into your account.

2.) Switch to your Author Fan Page.

Figure 22.13 – Switch to Author Fan Page

3.) Click "Create Call to Action."

Figure 22.14 – Call to Action

4.) Change the button to "Sign Up" and enter your e-mail

sign up URL.

5.) Done. Now people can sign up when they click

through your call to action.

Please note: If you wish to integrate your e-mail

collector into its own tab on your Facebook fan page (so

they can sign up on Facebook), you can.

For MailChimp:

Account Settings -> Integrations -> Facebook

For AWeber:

My Apps on the top bar of the dashboard -> Facebook

FREE GIFT

Promotional Check-List

Visit:

check-list.tkchapin.com

Subscribe to the Newsletter for special

Prices, free gifts and more!

www.tkchapin.com

AUTHOR'S NOTE

When you leave a review on a book you read, you're helping the author keep the lights on. Our books don't sell themselves, it's word of mouth and comments others have made. Simply visit Amazon and/or Goodreads and let others know how the book was for you. It'd help me greatly. Thank you!

ABOUT THE AUTHOR

BENJAMIN CHAPIN is an inspirational Christian author. He writes both fiction and non-fiction. His non-fiction titles are designed to help inspire those who are looking to improve all avenues of their life including: thinking, spiritual and financial.

Chapin gives all credit for his writing and storytelling abilities to God. The majority of his stories take place in and around his hometown of Spokane Washington. Chapin & his wife reside in Southeast Idaho and have three children. When not writing, he enjoys traveling, swimming and spending time with friends & family.

You can learn more about Benjamin by visiting his website www.benjaminchapin.com or you can learn more about his fiction visiting www.tkchapin.com.

www.ingramcontent.com/pod-product-compliance
Lightning Source LLC
Chambersburg PA
CBHW071335280526
45787CB00001B/111